Great
Instruction
Great
Achievement
for Students with Disabilities

A Road Map for Special Education Administrators

John L. O'Connor

COUNCIL OF ADMINISTRATORS
OF SPECIAL EDUCATION

Printed in the United States of America

ISBN: 978-1-58992-536-6

Council of Administrators of Special Education
Osigian Office Centre
101 Katelyn Circle
Suite E
Warner Robins, GA 31088
www.casecec.org

First Printing, 2016

This book is dedicated to Shawn, J.T., and Luke.

Contents

Acknowledgements

I would like to thank countless classroom teachers, students, parents, and educational leaders. By watching you, teaching with you, and leading with you, I have learned so much. I would also like to thank several people who have reviewed this book and been generous with their insights and suggestions. Their recommendations have been so helpful. Specifically, I extend my appreciation to Dr. Greg Benton, Ms. Lynn Pennington, Dr. Luann Purcell, Mr. Michael Remus, Mr. Aaryn Schmuhl, and Dr. Sarah West. Because of you, I am a better educator. Lastly, I would like to thank Brian O'Connor, an outstanding high school English teacher, who edited this book with a fine-tooth comb. There are some benefits to having a smarter, younger brother.

I
GREAT Instruction

Your superintendent calls you into the office. "Our results are clear. We have to drastically increase the achievement of students with disabilities. What should we do?"

Now is your time. As a special education administrator, you have this moment to make a big difference, to send a clear message and to change things for your students and your district. Are you ready?

At the end of the day, this is the ultimate question: How do we improve the learning and outcomes of our students? I have had the opportunity to ask that very question to thousands of special education administrators through various trainings and conversations over many years, and the responses were varied.

Increase parent involvement. Educate more students with disabilities in general education classes. Train principals. Provide ongoing professional development for teachers. Teach reading in all grades. Focus on improving IEPs.

All of those answers and many others are thoughtful and meaningful, but the answer is really very simple. If we want to increase the achievement of students with disabilities, we must *provide great instruction*. Great instruction is the answer. It is the only answer. In fact, great instruction will always be the answer. Student achievement standards will continue to evolve. Federal and state laws and regulations will continue to change. No matter. The answer to increasing student achievement will always be to *provide great instruction*.

What classes are we talking about? Across the country, roughly 62% of students with disabilities spend at least 80% of their school day in general education classes (U.S. Department of Education, 2014). In a school that has a six-period school day, that translates to the majority of students with disabilities attending five regular education classes. The numbers do not tell us anything about what happens in the classroom. There might be a co-teacher in the class or a behavior plan in place or assistive technology of some kind or there might be none of those things. In addition, another 20% of students with disabilities spend at least 40% of their school day in general education classes (U.S. Department of Education, 2014).

Therefore, if we are going to increase the achievement of students with disabilities, we must improve instruction in every class across the school. In fact, it is hard to find a class in most schools that does not include at least one student with an IEP. In order to increase the achievement of students with disabilities, we must provide great instruction at every school, in every class, for every student—every day.

The good news is that we, as educators, control 100% of the instruction. Great instruction occurs during the school day. As central office leaders, school principals, and teachers, we have direct access to the instruction. We own it. It is true that students experience a great deal when they are away from school, some good and some bad, but we, the educators, control the quality of instruction.

To tell you the truth, some students in our schools can be successful with a little less than great instruction. All students certainly deserve it, but some students come to our schools with great advantages in their learning. Some students even *teach themselves to read*. It usually occurs when they are three years old. Yesterday, Brenna was looking at a children's book, and all of those letters were squiggly lines. Today, she opens the book and all of those lines are letters. They now spell words, and those words tell a story.

Neurologically, it is amazing and it only happens to between 3-5% of children. To be honest, we don't have to throw the instruction ball too close to students such as Brenna; she and other students like her will pick it up and run with it, at least in the areas of reading. They certainly deserve great instruction, but they don't necessarily *need* it.

Our students with disabilities and many other students need great instruction. They cannot afford anything less.

That includes many students with disabilities and some students who come from economically disadvantaged situations, or those students who are learning English for the first time.

In addition, there are many students who struggle, but who don't qualify for any of our different categories. If you have been teaching longer than 16 seconds, you know that Leo and Marshall sit right next to each other. Leo has a disability and is served through an IEP. Marshall, on the other hand, did not qualify for special education services. In that classroom, however, both Leo and Marshall present in the same way. They both need very similar things instructionally. They both need great instruction.

So what is great instruction? Go ahead. Make a list. In five minutes, list those elements that define great instruction. You can even work with a partner. There is only a single rule: You can only write six bullets.

> If we are going to increase the achievement of students with disabilities, then we must provide GREAT instruction at every school, in every class, for every student— every day.

My List

When I ask this question in large-group training settings, I get lots of answers. Different participants, especially from different parts of the country, may use varied terminology, but they say essentially the same thing. At the end of the day, great instruction boils down to the following things.

It is:

- Research- or evidence-based,
- Measured,
- Rigorous,
- Geared toward performance standards, and
- Differentiated.

That covers a tremendous amount of ground, of course, but instruction should include all of these elements. There is, however, one missing piece—magic.

Magic happens when students eyes are flashing and they are fully enthralled with their work. For one outstanding primary school teacher, that magic happens when she takes her students to music class. She sneaks back to the classroom and places green, felt footprints on the classroom floor. When she leads her little students back to the classroom, she pauses in the hallway with great drama, "Oh no. You won't believe what happened. When we were out, a leprechaun stopped by and left a story on each of your desks. I don't think we should read it! What do you think?" The students respond in unison, "Yes. Let's read it!" (Eggers, 1993). That is magic.

At the middle-school level, students can be trained to work productively in small groups. Each youngster is engaged. The magnificent teacher slides back and observes. He knows when to skillfully approach a group and ask meaningful questions or provide scaffolded information. The bell can even ring. "Wait. Wait. We're not done yet!" That is magic.

Recently, I was told about a tremendous high school math teacher who has a "natural disaster" in her classroom every year (M. Wall, personal communication, 2015). The students enter the classroom and it is a mess. Desks are turned over and books and papers are spread all over the place. Sometimes it is a tsunami. Sometimes it is a tornado or hurricane. The students apply mathematical principles to analyze the force and magnitude of the disaster. They'll stop her in the hall and ask, "Is it going to happen today?" As you might expect, she feigns ignorance. Again, magic.

When you put all of the elements together, including magic, you get extremely powerful instruction. Using an acronym, we can think of GREAT instruction this way. It is:

- **G**uided by the performance standards;
- **R**igorous with **R**esearch-based practices;
- **E**ngaging and exciting;
- **A**ssessed continually to guide further instruction; and
- **T**ailored in flexible groups.

If we are going to increase the achievement and learning of our students with disabilities, then the first step is to provide GREAT instruction. Throughout the first half of this book, a visual organizer will be revealed. The content reflects the message that you can provide to your district superintendent, principals, teachers, and other school personnel who educate our students with disabilities. It is an instructional road map for increasing the achievement of students with disabilities over the next few years. The second half of the book will focus on the specific actions that you should undertake as a special education leader to help make GREAT instruction occur across your district and in all of your schools and classrooms.

Great Instruction = Great Achievement

Provide GREAT Instruction
(in every school, in every class, every day)

Guided by the performance standards

Rigorous with **R**esearch-based practices

Engaging and exciting

Assessed continuously to guide further instruction

Tailored in flexible groups

There is, however, a problem. If you asked 100 teachers what constitutes GREAT instruction, how many answers do you suppose you would get? Almost universally, the answer to that question is, "You would get 100 answers."

If GREAT Instruction is the path to increasing the achievement of students with disabilities, then we have to develop some consensus. Not only do we need to know the elements of GREAT instruction, as defined above, but we also need to agree what those elements look like and how to implement them across every classroom. For example, I define "tailored in flexible groups" in the following ways:

- We use "tailored" as a substitute for "differentiation" because the term differentiation has been used so widely that it has lost much of its meaning.
- Tailoring only occurs during small-group instruction. If large-group instruction is the dominant method observed in the classroom, tailoring is not occurring. All students are participating in the same activities, and therefore, the instruction is not different or differentiated.
- In every class, small-group instruction must occur routinely, at least 70% of the time. Typically, after third grade or so, we see much less small-group instruction. In high schools, we rarely see it. Small-group instruction must occur routinely in every class and in every grade.
- Small-group *instruction* is not the same thing as student *collaborative groups*. Collaborative groups are extremely powerful and often necessary; however, tailoring involves teacher-led instruction routinely provided for small groups.

- When there are two adults in the classroom, each adult should lead different instructional groups at the same time. This should be seen when there is a teacher and a paraprofessional in the same kindergarten classroom, for example, or when a general education and a special education teacher co-teach the same class or when any other arrangement involves two adults in the classroom.
- With small-group instruction, the teacher can alter the instruction for different learners; therefore, the students experience the instructional standard for that day in a way that is tailored to meet their needs.
- Likewise, the feedback the teacher gives the students can be tailored to respond to different students' attempts or practice turns. Essentially, both the students' practice turns and the feedback they receive can be increased and tailored to meet the students' instructional needs.
- Therefore, students participate in small, flexible instructional groups. There can also be independent student groups. Every student is actively participating in high rates of practice turns and receiving plenty of feedback.

Throughout this book, questions are provided for the members of the special education department. You might want to conduct a book study with your team. Sometimes, there are going to be questions interspersed within different chapters, and sometimes the questions appear at the end of the chapter. Your team can grow together as you read the different parts of this book and then brainstorm some useful answers to the **Guiding Questions**.

We know that increasing the achievement of students with disabilities through GREAT instruction will require deep partnerships among a variety of personnel, including central office staff, principals, assistant principals, and a wide variety of general education and special education teachers. In order for such a dispersed group of professionals to foster the deep commitment to collaboration that GREAT instruction requires, we must first arrive at a clear vision of what we can accomplish through GREAT instruction. This book represents the preparation and the homework needed in order for the special education department to support that change. Once you complete the book with your department, you might include others and re-read the first half. With your team prepared, you will be ready to facilitate the conversation and partnership.

Now, let's return to the topic of GREAT instruction to define each of its elements. The good news is you don't need to use my definition of "tailored in flexible groups." You should define the elements of GREAT instruction based on your own research and experiences.

Guiding Questions

Define each element of GREAT instruction. What are the non-negotiables that you *must* see to satisfy each element? What will you expect the teachers to be doing in the event each element is fully implemented in the classroom? What will the students be doing? What observable indicators would you expect to see? Include at least three bullets, but probably more, under each heading. GREAT instruction is:

- Guided by the performance standards:

- Rigorous:

- With Research-based practices:

- Engaging and exciting:

- Assessed continually to guide further Instruction:

- Tailored in flexible groups:

II
Research-Based Universal Instruction in Reading

An entire book could be written regarding each element of GREAT instruction. For now, however, let's focus only on the second "R" in GREAT instruction: research-based practices. If students with disabilities are going to meet high academic standards, our schools must routinely provide highly effective pedagogy in the form of research-supported practices. We cannot be satisfied with anything less. Under the umbrella of research-based instructional practices, we are going to divide our work under two headings: Research-based universal instruction (or Tier 1 Instruction) and Research-based specially designed instruction. The visual organizer presented earlier has been updated to include both categories.

Great Instruction = Great Achievement

Provide GREAT Instruction
(in every school,
in every class, every day)

Guided by the performance standards

Rigorous with Research-based
practices

Engaging and exciting

Assessed continuously to guide
further instruction

Tailored in flexible groups

Research-Based
Instructional
Practices

- Effective universal instruction In all content areas
- Specially designed instruction

Our students with disabilities must participate in effective instruction practices in every classroom. In fact, all students need that. Foundational Tier 1 or universal instruction is absolutely critical. Effective tiers of interventions or fantastic specially designed instruction, no matter how powerful, can never make up for ineffective universal instruction. Now, let's consider, as an example, effective universal instruction in reading.

Throughout my career in special education, I have had dozens and dozens of conversations with parents that go something like this: "My son Jeremiah is in fourth grade, and he is not reading as well as his brother who is a second grader. I want him to receive special education services and the school is telling me that he does not qualify. How do I get him into special education?"

This conversation has other variations. Sometimes, a school recommends that a student who struggles with reading should participate in special education services, but the family disagrees. While some families are seeking special education services and other families are very tentative to accept such services, those concerns are really not the core issue. The parents are worried because their child is having difficulty in learning how to read.

When you get that phone call or have that face-to-face conversation, and I am sure you do, how do you respond? Do you focus on the issue of special education eligibility, or do you address the underlying cause of concern: reading development? This is how I try to respond:

> "Ms. Johnson, do you mind if we put the issue of special education aside for a few minutes? Let's talk about Jeremiah's reading development. Do you mind if I explain how children typically develop reading skills? I will also ask you some questions about Jeremiah as we have the discussion. My disclaimer is that I haven't had the chance to meet Jeremiah, so I am not speaking specifically about him, but talking in generalities.
>
> "There are five big areas of reading development. When students are born, they immediately start to learn language. You started to talk to Jeremiah when he was born, and you continue to do so today. At first, he didn't understand the words, but over time he learned what some words meant and then started to use words himself. Every day, between birth through age four, when he started preschool, and then kindergarten, his language and vocabulary exploded. He learned lots of words, their meanings, and how to use them.
>
> "We see this development when young children understand what they hear and their talking becomes more developed. Can I ask you a question? When you see Jeremiah with other children his age, does he understand language to the same degree as those children? Does he speak and use words and sentences at the same level as his same-age friends?"

If Ms. Johnson shares that Jeremiah doesn't understand or speak at a commensurate level of other children his age, I ask more questions regarding language development. If Ms. Johnson shares that his receptive and expressive language are commensurate to other children, we move on to another component of reading development.

> "When children are three or four years old, they really start to learn to play with words. You probably sat next to him on the couch and read nursery rhymes or silly books. When children are that young, they are not really processing the print. They are looking at the pictures and listening to the sounds of the language and the words.
>
> "When you read a rhyming story, you would stress the rhymes. Eventually, children get used to hearing that pattern and start to anticipate

the rhyming words. The first sentence you read might have ended with "bat." Then the next sentence ended with "cat." They might guess "hat" or "pat." It doesn't even matter if a child guessed the correct word; the youngster is learning to rhyme. He is beginning to understand that two words sound the exact same, except the first sounds have changed.

"Then you read a silly story where many of the words started with the same sound. You may have read, 'Sally sold silly songs to Sue, Sarah, and Sam.' When you paused at the last word, the child might have guessed 'Cindy.' It doesn't matter that his guess wasn't the actual word in the story; he was starting to recognize that many words start with the same sound. If you noticed, I said the word 'Cindy.' When I said that word, you might have wondered why I chose a name that starts with the letter 'c.' Remember, I am not talking about letters, just the sounds in words. 'Cindy' starts with the same sound as 'Sally, silly, songs, and Sue.'

"As adults, it is almost impossible to think about words and the sounds without thinking about letters. When children are that young, they only know the sounds and learn that different words are merely sounds placed in different orders. They have sound discrimination. We call that ability to discriminate and manipulate sounds, *phonological awareness.* Some people refer to it as *phonemic awareness* to mean the same thing, even though there is a technical difference in those terms. For our purpose, we can say they mean the same thing.

"A 'phoneme' is the smallest sound in the English language. In fact, English has about 44 different sounds in the language. That's it. All of our words in English are made up of those 44 sounds. For example, the word 'pitch' ends with the /ch/ sound. Notice that I didn't say that the word ends with the letters 'c' and 'h.' The sound is /ch/ like you hear in the word chat. (When we write a phoneme, we put the corresponding letter or letters between forward slashes. So /b/ represents the b-sound, not the letter itself.)

> **Effective tiers of interventions or fantastic specially designed instruction, no matter how powerful, can never make up for ineffective universal instruction.**

"In order to learn how to read well, most children must build skills in listening and rearranging these sounds. Phonological awareness, or the awareness of all of these little sounds that make up words, is critical for most students. Can I ask you some questions about Jeremiah? If you say the following words, 'bat, cat, hat' and then pause for him to give you the next word, can he give you a rhyming word?

"If you give him several words that have the same beginning sound like 'man, munch, more, many' and then pause, will he give you a word that starts with the /m/ sound? If you ask him to clap the word 'dinosaur', can he clap out the syllables? That is another phonological awareness skill—the ability to hear the different syllables in words. Notice that none of these activities involve printed words. Phonological activities are done without looking at any written words or print. You only use your ears and your mouth.

"Let me tell you why that is important. At some point, usually when children are in pre-kindergarten, we start to introduce letters. A letter is really just a symbol, just like a Chinese character represents a concept, a letter in English represents a sound. The letter 'm' represents the /m/ sound. The letter 't' represents the /t/ sound.

"The problem starts when we show students letters and say, 'This is the letter "p." It says /p/.' If the student does not already know that the /p/ sound is only one sound in a larger system of sounds, then we have a problem. Even though the child may speak well and have a typical vocabulary, he might never have dissected words into sounds in a way that helps reading development. So, when you say, 'what sound does that make' or 'sound out that word', the student truly doesn't understand that there are tiny, individual sounds. He doesn't understand your question, and he can't explain that he doesn't understand. That lack of phonological awareness can be a big barrier.

"So far, we have talked about language development. For older students, part of that language is vocabulary development, one of the five dimensions of reading. We also talked about phonological awareness which is sound discrimination. The next skill needed in learning to read is phonics. That is when we start adding letters or symbols that represent sounds. At the beginning of this process, we tell preschoolers or kindergartners that this is the letter 'd' and it says the /d/ sound. Over time, we introduce all of the letters while we are putting short words together. We usually start with short words, such as cat, hat, dog, or mom. Children slowly learn how to decode and read words based on saying the sounds of each letter.

"Very often teachers teach children how to read using word families. They may start with the –at family. They put the letter 'h' in front and that makes the word 'hat'. Then the teacher adds the letter 'c' to –at and the students say the word 'cat'.

"Over time, a student's phonics or decoding skills grows from very simple, one-syllable words to complex words that might have more than one syllable. Some children have difficulty with phonics, and their limited decoding ability can become a problem with reading development. Can I ask you another question Ms. Johnson? When Jeremiah sees a word he doesn't know, what does he do?"

At this point in the conversation, a parent might tell me that the child doesn't know what to do. He makes sounds with his mouth, but they are not even close to the letters in the words, or Ms. Johnson might explain that Jeremiah usually says the first sound correctly, but then just makes up different sounds to guess the rest of the word. At other times, a parent might say that her child sounds out most words effectively, but does so very slowly. Each of these answers might indicate different instructional needs.

"It can also get a little tricky. Many times, teachers might suggest that a child is having difficulty with phonics, or decoding, when in fact he is missing the underlying skill of phonological awareness. Sometimes, he has phonological awareness, but is truly having difficulty with phonics.

"The next domain of reading development is oral reading fluency. Once children gain phonic skills, they start to read sentences, paragraphs, and stories. We want children to read orally with the appropriate speed and expression. We want their oral reading to be smooth, effortless, and have expression. For example, if the story says that a character whispers, we want them to whisper. If something in the story is exciting, we want their expression to reflect that excitement. We also want children to chunk different phrases or parts of sentences together. There is a fancy word to describe the appropriate rate and expression. That word is *prosody*. It means speaking in a conversational pattern—like we do when we speak to each other. We want children to read with the same pace and expression that they use when they speak with you. That is speaking with *prosody*.

"Unfortunately, some children read like robots. They might read one word at a time. Their reading is choppy and monotone. Such children pull words from the page, but only one at a time. They can decode the majority of words, but much of their energy is spent on the decoding process. They have little focus left to the actual meaning of the sentences or story. When children read in that halting way, they often don't comprehend what they are reading. They are devoting all of their thinking to decoding the words. They don't have the cognitive energy to think about what the passage is telling them.

"That difficulty with oral reading fluency often seems like difficulty with decoding, but sometimes it is not. It is difficulty with pulling the words off the page automatically, without effort, or without fluency. The student's thinking energy is focused on the letters in the word, not the meaning in the text. Ms. Johnson, when Jeremiah reads, does he read like a robot, with a halting pattern?

"The last domain is the real purpose for reading—reading comprehension. We want children to have a real understanding of what they read. All of those things I have discussed so far—language development that translates, in part, to vocabulary development, phonological awareness, phonics, and oral reading fluency—are just the building blocks to the real purpose of reading: to comprehend what we read.

"That goes from very simple in the latter parts of first grade where there are easier stories all of the way to the material that you and I read on a daily basis. We want children to know what the material means—what the material is about. At first, the stories are pretty literal. Then, as children mature, reading involves more inference: the ability to detect and interpret meaning that is only suggested or implied, not openly stated in the story.

"You are concerned about your son's reading. I want to make sure that we have some steps in place to help him. As his educators, we must identify his specific needs and then prescribe the exact instructional activities that are targeting those concerns, just like a doctor who prescribes the right medicine for someone's illness.

"I know that you want (or don't want) your child to receive special education services. Whether he ultimately qualifies or doesn't qualify for those services, I want to make sure we provide the right type of reading instruction that will help him become successful."

As this conversation continues with this parent, I tell them I am going to have someone from the school contact them to determine next steps. There are really two purposes for this conversation: First, I want the parent to have a general understanding of reading development because an informed parent is more effective at partnering with the school.

I also want to make sure that the main thing is the main thing. The mother is concerned about her child's reading ability. There certainly could be, and probably is, much more information to this situation. Whether or not the student later qualifies for special education, a student who has a reading deficit needs GREAT instruction that meets his needs. He needs quality instruction regardless of whether he experiences that instruction as part of an IEP or as part of general education. The most important thing is that we provide instruction that enables Jeremiah to become a proficient reader.

To be honest, this conversation should occur between *general education* personnel and the parent. We want all general education teachers in the primary and elementary grades to have great expertise in reading development. Unfortunately, that has not always been my experience. In addition, special education personnel who teach in our primary and elementary schools must *also* have great expertise, which is not always the case either.

It certainly does no harm for this discussion to occur between the special education department and the parent. I have had this discussion dozens and dozens of times in my career, but all of the information discussed above really includes effective, universal reading instruction, not specially designed instruction.

Every primary and elementary grade teacher (general *and* special education personnel) should have a deep understanding of the five dimensions of reading— vocabulary, phonological awareness, phonics, oral reading fluency, and reading comprehension (National Institute of Child Health and Human Development, 2000). As part of the research-based core instructional program in every kindergarten through fifth-grade class, teachers must be able to determine students' needs and how to implement effective instructional practices in each of those domains.

They also need the ability to explain the reading dimensions to parents. Almost without fail, the parents that I share this information with respond with, "Nobody has ever explained that to me." In some cases, they have searched for a number of years for answers regarding their child's reading development, and the professionals they have encountered have never articulated even the basics regarding reading development.

All students with disabilities, and any other student for that matter, need solid, foundational Tier 1 or universal reading instruction from general education personnel. Without that instruction, students' academic achievement will suffer. Students will be referred for interventions or special education, not because they struggle with their learning or because they have disabilities, but because they did not receive effective foundational instruction.

Literacy in All Content Areas and Grade Levels

Reading development, and really literacy development, does not end in elementary schools, nor is it limited to reading or English/language arts instructional blocks. Literacy development impacts all content areas and grade levels. It includes the ability to read, speak, listen, and write effectively.

The Common Core State Standards ensured that literacy development was placed at the forefront of educational priorities. In addition to developing standards in reading, English/language arts, and mathematics, literacy standards were provided in science, social studies, and technical subjects. This makes sense. If a student is truly literate in a content area, then the student is competent in that area. If Eric can read and understand biology text (including passages, numbers, graphs, tables, etc.), if he can write using the appropriate scientific terminology, and if he can express himself verbally at the appropriate level in biology, then Eric has demonstrated mastery in biology.

> In your school or school district, are all primary and elementary school teachers effective and systematic in providing instruction for youngsters in the five dimensions of reading? Are all principals and assistant principals effective at leading this work in their schools?

The Common Core State Standards have been adopted and incorporated into the state standards for the overwhelming majority of states. Even those few states that did not adopt the Common Core State Standards still include literacy standards for all grade levels and in the various content areas.

Unfortunately, many of our social studies, science, and technical subject teachers have not received ongoing training and support in literacy development. Even when they know their content, they don't possess the pedagogical skills to systematically improve their students' literacy development in that content area. We must ensure that robust and effective literacy instruction is provided at all grade levels across all content areas, from kindergarten through high school, as part of the universal instructional program.

Guiding Questions

- In your school or school district, are all primary and elementary school teachers effective and systematic in providing instruction for youngsters in the five dimensions of reading? Explain your answer.

- Are all primary and elementary principals and assistant principals effective at leading this work in their schools? Are the administrators acting as well-informed, instructional leaders in promoting effective reading instruction? Give examples to validate your response.

- How proficient are special education personnel in determining students' specific needs in the five dimensions of reading, and in systematically and strategically providing instruction? Do you have full and absolute confidence that the teachers effectively determine students' needs in those five domains and then take the most effective next steps regarding instruction? Explain your answer.

- What about special education administrators in your office? If a special education coordinator or the special education director received Mrs. Johnson's phone call, would he or she have the reading background to speak with the parent? Does he or she ensure that reading instruction is being provided with great expertise and fidelity for students with disabilities? Provide evidence for your response.

- Have your general education teachers in all content areas been provided ongoing professional development that included coaching and monitoring regarding effective literacy instruction within their content area? Provide a rationale for your response.

- Are you confident that all content-area teachers in your school or district demonstrate great expertise in providing literacy instruction on a routine basis?

- If the answers to any of the questions above are "no," what steps will you take to address the need? Remember, it is helpful to prioritize action steps because you cannot address everything in one fell swoop.

III
Core Instruction in Mathematics and Other Content Areas

Effective universal or Tier 1 instruction is certainly not limited to reading, English/language arts, or literacy in content areas. Let's turn our attention to mathematics. How do we increase the mathematics achievement of our students?

That's a tough question. In my career in public education since 1990, the pendulum has swung wildly. We have swung back and forth in a variety of areas:

- From completely teacher-led instruction to student-centered instruction.
- From teachers using models and careful explanations to students developing their own strategies.
- From an almost exclusive focus on procedures, such as the "traditional" procedure for long division, to an almost exclusive emphasis on math concepts underlying mathematics.

So back and forth swings the pendulum. Where should we land? Should teachers lead instruction or should students find their own way? Should teachers instill procedural algorithms or illuminate the underlying concepts? Again, tough questions.

Fortunately, we have some answers. In 2006 the President issued an executive order to create a panel of experts, the National Mathematics Advisory Panel (2008), who would try to answer some of these challenging questions and many other elements that impact math achievement. Their charge was to make recommendations "based on the best available scientific evidence" (p. A1–A2). In my mind, one reason the President created this group was to stop the continuous swinging of the pendulum; to provide once and for all some evidence-based conclusions regarding the nature of effective math instruction.

In all, the panel published 45 recommendations and findings on a wide variety of topics related to improving math achievement. The panel's recommendations focused on enabling all students to be fully equipped to enter and complete high school algebra (usually referred to as Algebra I and Algebra II). The report indicates that "students who complete Algebra II are more than twice as likely to graduate from college than students with less mathematical preparation" (p. xiii). Therefore, to facilitate this outcome, many of the recommendations concentrated on how to better prepare pre-kindergarten through middle-school students for success in algebra.

For our purposes, we will review only those recommendations that lend themselves to Tier 1, universal and core instructional practices (all terms meaning the same thing) for all students.

Should Universal Instruction Focus on Conceptual Understanding, Problem Solving, or Computational Fluency?

In mathematics education, as in reading instruction, there have been battles waged over *what* should be taught to school children. In one camp, various professionals recommend focusing on procedures and algorithms which also ensures that students know their "basic facts." This approach is often supported by adults who remember their math classrooms.

At the other extreme, some professionals have argued for an approach that increases the focus on students' conceptual understanding while minimizing instruction in computational fluency or algorithmic procedures. To this end, some professionals have even claimed that it is actually *harmful* to teach students "standard American algorithms." So, which is it?

Best practices actually include all of those things. According to the National Mathematics Advisory Panel, students need instruction in conceptual understanding, problem solving, *and* computational fluency. They are all interconnected and necessary.

> *Debates regarding the relative importance of these aspects of mathematical knowledge are misguided. These capabilities are mutually supportive, each facilitating learning of the others. Teachers should emphasize these interrelations; taken together, conceptual understanding of mathematical operations, fluent execution of procedures, and fast access to number combinations jointly support effective and efficient problem solving.* (p. xix)

How about that? We actually need balance. Our classrooms should include all three. We must help students understand the underlying concepts of mathematics, and we must deliver effective instruction in procedures and algorithms. In addition, we must provide instructional experiences that enable students to develop mathematical problem-solving skills.

We shouldn't focus exclusively on procedures. Historically, however, much of our math instruction has done exactly that. Unfortunately, if our students learn to divide a multi-digit number that includes a decimal by another multi-digit number without understanding what division represents or how the two numbers interact with each other, then our students are not developing mathematical thinking.

On the other hand, if we exclusively focus on developing mathematical concepts, and applying those concepts to the context of problem solving without teaching students how to use efficient and automatic procedures—like the traditional long division procedure, for example—then we are likewise failing to meet the panel's recommendations.

The question is not which element to preserve and which element to abandon. It shouldn't be an "or" question. The components are not mutually exclusive. Effective universal instruction in mathematics includes all three. We should provide instructional experiences that enable students to develop conceptual understanding, problem solving, *and* computational fluency.

In fact, all three components complement one another. Students can understand the underlying concepts of mathematics, apply those concepts to meaningful problems, and demonstrate efficient computation through standard algorithms. The teacher should help the students connect all three of these so that students understand their interconnectedness and how they often represent one another. With universal instruction, we can stop the pendulum from swinging any longer.

Should Instruction Be Teacher Directed or Student Centered?

Much like the historic controversy described above, there have been consistent disagreements about which is more productive: teacher-led instruction or student-directed activities.

Should teachers set a systematic course of instruction and primarily deliver that instruction, or should students choose activities and navigate their own learning? As you might expect based on the recommendations of the panel above, we need balance. Both of those approaches are needed and neither should be used exclusively. The panel summarized it nicely when they wrote the following:

> *All encompassing recommendations that instruction should be entirely "student centered" or "teacher directed" are not supported by research. If such recommendations exist, they should be rescinded. If they are being considered, they should be avoided. High-quality research does not support the exclusive use of either approach.*

That is pretty strong and direct language. We need to quit arguing about which method is superior because, according to the research, students need both. Teachers must certainly provide instruction to students and create sequences of instructional experiences, and we also need to provide students the opportunity to investigate and solve mathematical challenges without teacher-driven instruction. Again, students need both.

Let's step away from the swinging pendulum for a moment. Some of the recommendations of the panel really support what teachers have known for quite some time. Many math teachers will tell you that fractions are a challenging subject for many students, no matter the grade level; in consequence, the next recommendation from the panel should not be at all surprising.

Effective instruction in fractions (and related percentages and decimals) is critical as trouble with fractions is commonplace.

After surveying many teachers and reviewing student achievement data, the panel recognized that a tremendous number of American students have difficulty with fractions. This difficulty creates a significant barrier to students becoming successful in Algebra I and II. As mentioned above, instruction should include the mutually supportive areas of conceptual understanding, problem solving, and computational fluency regarding fractions.

It is particularly helpful to represent fractions on a number line. That makes sense, right? Fractions, percentages, and decimals are merely quantities just like any other number that rests on the number line. Unfortunately, in our elementary schools, fraction representations are often limited to circles, pizzas, and pies. Those representations have their place, but they really don't demonstrate the quantity of fractions as well as when number lines are used.

The results of formative assessments should be used to guide ongoing instruction.

The "A" in the acronym GREAT instruction stands for *Assessed continuously to guide further instruction.* This notion of assessment applies to all content areas, including mathematics as recommended by the National Mathematics Advisory Panel.

Although I might never have met you, if you are an educator past a certain age, I know how you were taught spelling. What happened on Monday? You received a list of new words. What happened on Tuesday, Wednesday, and Thursday? You completed different activities with those spelling words. You wrote them in sentences, played games with them, and applied them in various ways. (Some of those instructional activities were ineffective, but that is for a different discussion.) What about Friday? That's right—a spelling test.

And what happened the following Monday? All students received a new list of spelling words. In fact, all students in the class received the same new list of spelling words. What about that spelling test? What was that for? Unfortunately, it was used to put a score in the teacher's grade book, nothing more.

The results of those spelling tests could have provided the teacher some powerful information. By using effective error analysis, the teacher could have determined whether or not there were common misunderstandings across a large number of students, whether or not some students needed additional instruction over a specific spelling skill, or whether or not individual students needed additional support. The error analysis might also have revealed that some students were ready for more challenging spelling words.

In our language arts classrooms of the past, teachers used ongoing assessments primarily for grading students, not for analyzing their needs and then determining effective next steps for instruction. As educators, we must make effective assessment analysis a regular part of universal instruction so we can determine the best next steps—not only for the entire class but also for different groups and for individuals within the class.

Sometimes, the ongoing analysis of data reveals that the instruction should be improved. When many students in the class are not meeting the instructional standards, then perhaps the instruction was not as efficient or as effective as it could have been.

In all of our classes, including mathematics classes as recognized by the National Mathematics Advisory Panel, the ongoing analysis of data should be used to drive continued instruction. This can be extremely powerful to increasing student achievement. The panel did recognize, however, that many teachers may not know how to effectively analyze the data or how to connect those results to effective instructional next steps. Therefore, many teachers need ongoing professional development and support in learning how to analyze the data and how to plan and implement instruction that responds to the analysis.

> **Should universal instruction in mathematics focus on conceptual understanding, problem solving, or computational fluency? Best practice actually includes all of three.**
>
> National Mathematics Advisory Panel (2008)

The recommendations provided by the National Mathematics Advisory Panel certainly do not describe an exhaustive list of every element needed in an effective math classroom, but they do provide solid information regarding instructional activities that should be included. If we are going to increase achievement of students with disabilities in the area of mathematics—or of any student for that matter—then we must ensure that universal instruction involves strong research-based practices.

Effective Core Instruction in All Content Areas

In addition to effective instruction in reading, literacy, and mathematics, we must ensure that all students receive research-based instructional practices in all of their courses. In your school district, has there been a consistent and diligent focus on improving pedagogy across schools and across content areas?

Fortunately, there is an ever-expanding body of knowledge regarding effective instructional practices that can be implemented across a variety of content areas. For example, Marzano, Pickering, & Pollock (2001) published a meta-analysis of instructional practices that were linked to increased student learning. The effective instructional practices were:

- *Identifying similarities and differences*
- *Summarizing and note taking*
- *Reinforcing effort and providing recognition*
- *Homework and practice*
- *Nonlinguistic representations*
- *Cooperative learning*
- *Setting objectives and providing feedback*

- *Generating hypotheses*
- *Questions, cues, and advance organizers*

That original book has been updated (Dean, Hubb, Pitler, & Stone, 2013). Another example includes the work of Hattie (2008), who conducted comprehensive meta-analyses that rated a wide variety of instructional practices and other elements based on effect size on student learning.

These works give educators a great opportunity. We can take a step back and analyze the instruction that we are consistently providing in our classrooms. Then we can determine if we are implementing pedagogy that has been shown to have a positive impact on student achievement. If not, we have the research to make adjustments to our instruction.

In each of our districts, we should make it a top priority to implement those instructional practices that have the greatest probability of impacting student learning for all students, including students with disabilities. If we allow hunches and personal preferences to shape our instruction, instead of research-based pedagogy, many of our students will not experience increased achievement. We must therefore look to the research in order to build strong core instructional programs in all content areas.

Guiding Questions

- In your schools, is effective research-based core instruction routinely provided in mathematics as described by the National Mathematics Advisory Panel? Are teachers familiar with the recommendations of the panel and are ongoing professional development systems in place to delve deeply into those recommendations? Provide a rationale for your answer.

- Does the core Tier 1 instruction (or universal instruction) include a mutual and inter-related focus on conceptual understanding, problem solving, and computational fluency? If not, what can be done to include all three elements?

- Is there a balance between teacher-directed and student-led instructional activities or has one of those approaches been primarily promoted in your district? If there is a need for balance, how can greater balance be achieved?

- Is there an intensive instructional and cohesive focus on improving students' capacity with fractions, percentages, and decimals that includes conceptual understanding, computational fluency, and problem solving across grade levels? Are fractions taught routinely using number lines (in addition to other methods)? If not, what steps should be taken to improve this?

- Are ongoing formative student data used to systematically drive instruction? What processes are in place in which teachers implement and review ongoing student work, performance, and data to drive next instructional steps? Are teachers meeting together routinely to analyze student work and collaboratively make instructional decisions based on the student efforts? How are school administrators involved in this process? If your answers are less than desirable, what next steps can be implemented to move this work forward?

- Has the district chosen specific research-based instructional practices to implement in all content areas? If not, what can be done to do so?

- Is there an effective professional development system in place to promote those high probability instructional practices? Does the professional development system include training, ongoing support or coaching, and teacher or leader continual brainstorming and debriefing in order to refine and perfect implementation of the instructional practices? Provide examples to support your answer.

- When high probability instructional practices are implemented, do teachers and leaders work together to analyze student work to determine if students are learning at high levels? Describe the activities that occur.

IV
Specially Designed Instruction

It is critical that students with disabilities participate in effective core instruction, but the same can be said for all students. Students with disabilities, however, also need instruction that meets their unique needs resulting from their disability. They need specially designed instruction.

In fact, since 1975 (Education for all Handicapped Children's Act), special education has been defined as *specially designed instruction . . . to meet the unique needs of a child with a disability.* Even though the legislation has been reauthorized and updated multiple times in the 40 or so years since its original passage (IDEA 1990; IDEA 1997; IDEIA 2004), the definition of special education has not changed. As stated earlier, the second "R" in the acronym GREAT stands for *research-based practices*, which includes both effective universal instruction and specially designed instruction. In this chapter, we will review the latter.

Great Instruction = Great Achievement

Provide GREAT Instruction
(in every school,
in every class, every day)

Guided by the performance standards

Rigorous with Research-based practices

Engaging and exciting

Assessed continuously to guide further instruction

Tailored in flexible groups

Research-Based
Instructional
Practices

- Effective universal instruction in all content areas

- Specially designed instruction

Since *specially designed instruction* has been in the federal legislation for several decades, let's start with an obvious question: What is *specially designed instruction?* Develop a description that reflects your practical experiences and best insights. You can even work with a team.

Guiding Questions

- What is specially designed instruction? Try to limit your response to a maximum of six bullets.

Your description of *specially designed instruction* might include the following descriptors. It:

- Is specific to the individual student.
- Is designed to meet the unique needs of a student with a disability.
- Is research-based.
- Is described in the IEP.
- Enables the student to meet grade-level standards.
- Includes alterations in the content, methodology, and delivery of instruction.

All of those elements are certainly accurate, and they are legally true. Unfortunately, there is a problem. They are not very descriptive. In fact, for teachers who are charged with providing specially designed instruction, those descriptors have very limited value. As a teacher, what *specific* instructional practices should I implement? What instructional practices should sit on top, or coordinate with, a student's universal instruction?

After 40 plus years in the federal legislation, there still isn't a national consensus on what instructional practices constitute specially designed instruction. I know part of the barrier. Specially designed instruction must meet the unique needs of each student with a disability, and every student is unique. Two children with disabilities, even the same disability, can have very different needs.

So we ask each of our special education teachers to analyze the needs of each and every student, including the intricacies of their disabilities. Then each of our special education teachers must research the applicable instructional practices and determine which practice has the greatest probability of increasing the student's achievement. Finally, each teacher must implement those practices with near absolute fidelity, usually in a general education classroom. In addition to all this, each teacher must complete all of the special education compliance activities and all "other duties as assigned." Sound reasonable? No.

We need to provide more support and direction for our special education teachers, and for our regular education teachers as well. We cannot expect them to start with a blank slate every time they enroll a new student with a disability.

How can we provide more support to our teachers? Let's refine our scope a bit. For the purpose of the discussion in this book, let's not focus on all students with disabilities. Let's focus on those students with disabilities who are pursuing grade-level standards—the youngsters whom we are striving to help meet the same standards as other students.

Across the population of students with disabilities in our schools, that group includes the overwhelming majority of students. In fact, only a very small percentage of students with disabilities are pursuing alternate achievement standards. Those students are taking alternative assessments and are not participating in the typical assessments, nor do they have the same academic expectations as other students. These are the students with the most significant cognitive disabilities. Let's focus on the great majority of students with disabilities who are pursuing grade-level performance standards, not those participating in alternative assessments.

Does the job description for the special education teacher detailed earlier sound a little more reasonable now? Perhaps not yet. Don't worry. We'll get there.

Defining Specially Designed Instruction

Can we make a list of instructional practices that, if implemented effectively and with fidelity, would increase the achievement of a large majority of students with disabilities? I think we can.

Think about the wide variety of students with disabilities who are pursuing grade-level achievement standards. Are there instructional practices that, if implemented, would have a positive impact on their achievement? With a partner, or a group of colleagues, make a list. What instructional practices are needed by the greatest number of students with disabilities?

Guiding Questions

- Make a list of instructional practices that are needed by the greatest majority of students with disabilities who are pursuing grade-level standards. Try to limit your list to six or seven bullets.

My List

Here is my list. It may differ from yours, which is certainly acceptable. In my opinion, if we are going to increase achievement, most students with disabilities need the following instructional practices (on top of effective universal instruction). As educators, we need to:

- Drastically increase practice turns and feedback.
- Provide explicit instruction.
- Provide explicit and embedded vocabulary instruction.
- Implement fill-the-gap interventions.
- Incorporate metacognitive instruction.
- Implement effective behavioral systems.

Are all of these research-based practices beneficial for the vast majority of students with disabilities? If they were implemented with great fidelity across every classroom, for every student with a disability, would we see increased student achievement? I think so.

Does that then mean that they are *needed* by students with disabilities? I would say yes. If these specific research-based instructional practices are needed by the vast majority of students with disabilities, then perhaps they set the foundation of *specially designed instruction.*

It is ok with me if you have a different list. You may replace one or more of these practices with something else. I am fine with that. I certainly don't think I have the knowledge, nor the authority, to make a list that meets the needs of every school district or school in the country. My point is this: For your school or for your district, you need a list. If you do not have a similar list, you are not providing sufficient support for your general and special education teachers. More importantly, your students with disabilities are not participating in the instruction they need.

> Can we make a list of instructional practices that if implemented effectively and with fidelity, would increase the achievement of a large majority of students with disabilities? I think we can.

My list sets the *foundation* for specially designed instruction. Some students will need participation in specific instructional practices that are not listed. This list, and whatever list you develop, is certainly not exhaustive. It is not meant to be. It reflects the starting point for specially designed instruction for students with disabilities across your district who are pursuing the same level of standard proficiency as non-disabled students. Now, let's discuss the different components of the list.

Before proceeding, please understand there is a disclaimer. The descriptions below are very brief and incomplete. They are meant to be a cursory introduction only to some of the information available about these instructional practices. If you do choose to use any of them in your school district, please research them deeply and carefully in order to fully support your teachers and school leaders.

Drastically Increase Practice Turns and Feedback

The longer my career in public education, the more I think that all learning is ultimately a result of practice turns and feedback. It does not matter if you are learning to ballroom dance, crochet a sweater, speak a foreign language, compute long division, or build a bookcase. People learn by making attempts and receiving feedback.

We see the importance of practice turns and feedback in the realms of athletics, academics, the fine arts, and in any other field that includes demonstration of skill and knowledge. If you ask virtually anyone how you get better at playing the piano (or blocking a tackle, solving equations, or singing a solo), the answer is invariably, "practice, practice, practice." Any teacher, coach, professor, or construction worker will tell you that you get better at a skill by doing that skill.

Practice turns can occur when students are dissecting an earthworm, analyzing historical documents from World War II, or when a group of dancers repeat the same series of dance moves in order to perfect their technique, rhythm, and emotional expressiveness. Practice turns also happen when students are working on a math task as a group and are deeply engrossed in finding multiple paths to a solution.

Practice turns, regardless of the terminology that is used, are certainly not limited to low-level skills.

Practice, however, is certainly not enough. There is the old saying, "practice makes perfect," but that saying has been updated and corrected, "*perfect* practice makes perfect." That may be a little extreme, but it illustrates a point. Practicing something without feedback has risks. Any little league baseball coach will tell you that he would prefer to teach an eight-year-old player who has never tossed his first pitch how to throw a ball than to teach a more experienced player who has already learned poor technique. Without feedback, many people develop poor habits. Such risks make ongoing and effective feedback critical to achievement.

So where can school children get feedback? In a classroom, there are four main sources. Students can receive feedback from: an adult, peers, technology, or from themselves. We have all seen teachers provide feedback to students, unfortunately, some good and bad. All feedback must be informative. It is much better to say, "That is correct because you summarized the most important parts of the paragraph," than to say, "That is correct."

Sometimes, that feedback can take the form of questions or guidance. "If someone else thought that your argument was limited in some way, what limitations would they likely mention?" As the adults in our schools, we need to provide helpful and informative feedback.

All feedback does not need to come from the teacher. In fact, that would make an extremely ineffective learning environment. Students can be great sources of feedback for one another. Many times this occurs when children work in collaborative groups or informally help one another. It can also happen in well-planned and structured situations like Peer-Assisted Learning Strategies (Fuchs & Fuchs, 2005) or Cross-Age Peer Tutoring (O'Connor, Primm & Stancil, 2006). Students are an extremely valuable source of feedback for one another.

I would be remiss if we didn't mention the feedback that technology can provide. That feedback can range from somewhat simple (and necessary) like the indication of spelling errors or the indication that an attempt is right or wrong (i.e., Quizlet®), or the feedback from technology can be much more sophisticated. The application ST Math®, for example, provides nonverbal, visual feedback that is informative. It not only indicates why an attempt is inaccurate but it also reveals visually why it is inaccurate conceptually. Likewise, it also affirms students' attempts, when correct, by showing virtual manipulatives that indicate the concepts underpinning the mathematics.

Some computer applications allow for students to create products to illustrate their level of mastery of the material. When a student is building a product using the technology, she continually reviews what is being built (i.e., a game) to determine if it is performing in the way she intended. That feedback guides her next attempts.

Lastly, students can provide feedback to themselves. This skill develops as students mature and become more adept at a particular body of knowledge. Students who are talented writers can read their own work and realize that the rhythm is off. Students who are skillful in robotics can re-examine a circuit when the desired movement is not functioning properly. Gifted singers know that their aria is weak and determine the next steps for improvement.

Even though it is a skill developed over time, we model that for our youngest children: "You took Bobby's toy. Was that nice? What should you have done?" We also help children use this skill as they grow: "After you finish your writing assignment, use the rubric to evaluate your work."

Students who struggle and students with disabilities are often at a disadvantage when it comes to practice turns and feedback. First of all, when a student struggles with a concept or subject matter, he invariably needs many more practice turns and much more systematic feedback in order to gain skillfulness. In fact, virtually all special educators would agree that students with disabilities have a much greater need for practice turns and feedback than other learners. If a typical student can learn a new skill with ten practice turns, a student with a disability may need many, many more attempts at that skill while also receiving informative and guiding feedback.

This just makes sense, and you see a variation of this in the world of athletics. Ask any coach. Some youngsters just have natural talent in a sport. They certainly must work hard and be devoted to practice, but they are ahead of many other athletes in that they can master a skill with fewer practice turns than less gifted athletes.

So students with disabilities need more practice turns in their weak content areas. Unfortunately, many of our students with disabilities actually get far fewer attempts than other students. Yes, the students who need the highest number of practice turns and feedback usually get the fewest. We have many students with disabilities who have learned the great skill of being invisible. They often sit about three-quarters back in the typical classroom. They don't bring attention to themselves, and they have this unspoken arrangement with the teacher. If you don't call on me, I won't cause any trouble.

Teachers are often unknowing partners with this transaction. With twenty-five or more students in many classrooms, it is hard "to see" these students. They become invisible. The students don't answer questions. They don't volunteer to lead groups. They don't get engaged in those healthy discussions or debates in class. They don't disagree when a student or teacher says something that doesn't make sense, and they certainly don't ask for help.

When the students are assigned independent work, they are masters at pretending they are engaged, but their apparent engagement is an act, a survival mechanism. They often don't understand the work, and they don't want the other students or the teacher to understand that they don't understand.

These students are invisible and they take very few practice turns and receive very little feedback. Again, the youngsters who need the greatest number of practice turns take the fewest. The students who genuinely need the most explicit and targeted feedback receive the least.

There are other students with disabilities who also receive fewer practice turns and less academic feedback. Many students with disabilities have avoidance behaviors that interfere with their active engagement in attempts. The avoidance behaviors may be disruptive and lead to behavioral corrections, referrals to the office, or disciplinary suspensions.

Some other students have behaviors, though perhaps not as disruptive, which interfere with practice turns. Their lack of organizational skills or executive functioning skills is so profound that much of their time is devoted to finding their materials, running back to their lockers, or getting themselves organized. They may look very active, but the actual time they devote to practice turns is actually very short.

What can we do to drastically increase practice turns and feedback for all students, but most importantly, for students with disabilities? First, we have to notice. When we walk in a classroom, we need to take our eyes off of the teacher and focus on the students. Are all students receiving a high number of practice turns and feedback? Sometimes the answer is no, and it is not because some specific students avoid class participation. Limited practice turns and feedback can be a result of the teacher's design of the instructional activity.

I recently spent some time in a kindergarten classroom. A school administrator requested that I observe a youngster who was having consistent behavioral problems. During the lesson, that student was doing fine, and isn't that often the case? Sometimes a student who has behavioral challenges demonstrates engaged and positive behavior when that observer enters the room. Even if the observer successfully disguises his purpose for being there, the dynamic changes slightly. The novelty of having another adult in the room, especially an adult who is new to the children, alters the student's typical behavior. (Or, sometimes, the student's behavior is not as problematic as the teacher indicated.)

Even though that youngster was performing nicely and did not exhibit any negative behavioral challenges, I noticed something else. There was not a high rate of practice turns or feedback. The kindergarten teacher, who has many positive skills, was leading carpet time.

Each child was sitting on his or her square in the carpet, and the teacher was leading a math activity. She was showing various cards that displayed groups of dots. Ms. Duffy asked the students, "When you see these dots, how do you group them to determine how many dots there are? Sarah, what do you think?" Then Sarah would say something like, "There are nine dots. First I see those five and then I see those four. That makes nine dots."

> The longer my career in public education, the more I think that all learning is ultimately a result of practice turns and feedback. It doesn't matter if you are learning to ballroom dance, crochet a sweater, speak a foreign language, compute long division, or build a bookcase. People learn by making attempts and receiving feedback.

Ms. Duffy replied, "Very good, Sarah. Does anyone have another way?" Then different children were called upon to share how they grouped the dots visually in order to determine how many dots were on the page. The teacher spent several minutes showing different cards and asking children to explain their approach.

As different children attempted this task, she provided meaningful feedback. She used her fingers on the cards to demonstrate what each child was saying and then offered either confirmative or corrective feedback. After around 15 minutes, the task changed to identifying different shapes, but the process stayed the same. "Rodney, what do you think? Now Sandi, you try it."

As I watched this lesson for roughly 35 minutes, I began to count different students' practice turns. During that 35 minutes of class time, each child had approximately three attempts at the different tasks and received individual feedback from Ms. Duffy.

There was also a kindergarten paraprofessional in the classroom. During carpet time, the paraprofessional—we'll call her Ms. Logan—was preparing the rest of the classroom for the next scheduled activity—center time. She was placing different materials at different tables around the room so that students could rotate through the activities.

I had two reactions to this observation, and I am certainly not being critical of Ms. Duffy nor Ms. Logan. They had a well-managed classroom and spoke wonderfully to the students. But I did notice during that 35-minute period that each student only averaged about three practice turns followed by individual feedback from the teacher. That is really a suppressed number of practice turns for all students, and especially students who struggle. Who was getting the most practice turns and feedback in the room? The teacher! She had dozens of attempts during those 35 minutes. In addition, students would respond to her statements with acknowledgements or additional questions. They were giving her feedback after she shared her thought. The teacher who already has competence in the skills actually was taking more practice turns and receiving more feedback than any of the students. That doesn't make sense, does it?

How could we alter the lesson so that students receive more practice turns and more feedback? What if the teacher offered practice turns to all students at the same time and also relied on the students to provide feedback to one another? Ms. Duffy could model the activity. Then, she could hold up the next card and say, "Now it is your turn. Look at this card. How would you group the dots to find the total? Don't say anything yet. Get the answer in your head." As a good teacher, she would give the appropriate wait time.

"Now, turn to your partner. Red Bird students, tell your Blue Bird partner how you grouped the dots to find the answer." After a few minutes, "Now Blue Birds, tell your Red Bird partners how you grouped the dots. Now students, raise your hand if your *partner* grouped it like..."

Do you see how Ms. Duffy's activity can be shifted slightly, with no additional work for her, so that every student gets a turn for every card that is raised? Instead of three or so turns in 35 minutes, every student gets many more turns and then receives feedback from their classmates and Ms. Duffy.

Of course, this approach to the activity takes some student training. Students who are paired will need to have some type of cue about which partner goes first (like the Red Bird – Blue Bird example above). The teacher will also need to pace it effectively so students have enough time for a practice turn without problematic excess time. But, with a little training and forethought, this very common activity can be ramped up considerably.

What about Ms. Logan? During this observation, there was a second adult who was completing organizational tasks. What if she became involved in the lesson and took a group of students to another location in the room? Ms. Duffy could have a group and then Ms. Logan could have a group.

Let's say there are 24 kindergarten students in this class. When the children are separated for carpet time, then the teacher-student ratio is immediately cut in half. Now there is one adult for 12 students in the group. Even if they preserve the original lesson without any other improvements, each student now receives twice the amount of practice turns and feedback from the teacher. If they split the students into two groups *and* approach the activity as suggested, then you *dramatically* increase practice turns and feedback. Now, we are having some real impact on student learning.

Whenever there are two adults in the room, whether they are a kindergarten teacher paired with a paraprofessional or a general education teacher co-teaching with a special education teacher or even a teacher paired with a Title I push-in teacher, both should routinely lead small groups. Even if the teachers choose not to modify the lesson to increase the frequency of practice turns, the number of practice turns and amount of subsequent feedback are doubled.

Something else happens as well. The type of practice turns and feedback are often differentiated or tailored. When there is a smaller student-teacher ratio, the adults naturally alter the practice turns and feedback to meet individual student's needs. With fewer students, the adult is able to observe more closely the attempts made by the students and then alter the feedback and following practice turns accordingly.

I am certainly not picking on kindergarten teachers nor on Ms. Duffy specifically. On the contrary, kindergarten and first-grade teachers are usually much more proficient at providing practice turns and feedback along with small-group instruction than teachers of older students. They very often provide stations around the room where students receive high rates of practice. They also sit with small groups of students at the kidney table and work individually with every student multiple times over the course of the week.

All teachers, regardless of the age of their students, should drastically increase student practice turns and feedback. We have discussed two major approaches to do just that: 1) design activities so that students make attempts and receive feedback at the same time, and 2) enlist all adults in a classroom in the delivery of instruction to small, flexible groups. Rotating independent student groups can also be utilized in classrooms that include more than one adult. That increases practice turns and feedback even further.

What does this look like in a class for older students? The same approaches can apply. Let's say that Mr. Morris' class is orally reading a novel of historical fiction. Instead of having each student taking turns orally reading, students could group into pairs. They can take turns orally reading. Just with this slight alteration to the lesson, students go from receiving one or maybe two practice turns of oral reading to reading aloud for half the instructional time.

If you pair the students strategically, then a student who orally reads with great fluency and expression can be paired with a student who struggles with those skills. By listening to the more fluent reader, Jose, who struggles with those skills, will start to read with greater expression and fluency.

After the oral reading activity is over, the paired students can then compare the novel's plot developments to the informational text read the previous day. The pair of students can then choose to answer any five of the ten presented questions. "Students, each of you must complete any five of the questions about our two reading selections. Remember to cite your sources correctly. Decide with your partner which five of the questions to answer."

"Using your visual organizer, write your answer to the first question independently. I will give you five minutes. Then discuss your answers with your partner. After your discussion, complete the section titled *Thoughts I am adding after discussions with my partner*."

Think of the constant student practice turns and peer feedback in this classroom activity. Isn't this approach more productive than the two other options: students working independently or students working in groups where one or two students do much of the work? With this design, everyone gets plenty of practice, each student receives peer feedback, and all students respond to the feedback by recording additional thoughts.

The student partnerships should not be set in stone. Every few weeks, Mr. Morris assigns new partners so students have the opportunity to receive a wide variety of perspectives and feedback. He will certainly be intentional in how he assigns partners.

With just a little tinkering of the instructional design, the number of practice turns and feedback can be drastically increased. When I pop into classrooms for a quick observation, either formally or informally, I immediately look for practice turns and feedback. That is always the first thing I notice. It tells me more about the class than any other indicator.

At the middle or high school, the suppressed practice turns and feedback often look differently. I see teachers lecturing from the front of the room and then giving assignments for the students to complete. During a lecture, the person who is getting the highest rate of practice turns is the teacher. She is demonstrating a skill or explaining concepts, and she is getting feedback from her students in the form of questions, affirmations, or responses to her questions. On the other hand, the students who are not volunteering to answer questions or who are struggling are not participating in the number of practice turns that are necessary to gain competence.

Some could argue that under this scenario it is the assignment that delivers to each student a high rate of practice turns. While that may be the case, the assignment itself offers little to no feedback. So many practice turns with minimal feedback can be counterproductive, like a little leaguer teaching himself how to throw a fast ball. As students are learning a new skill, and even when they are engaging with that skill at a deeper level, they need tons of insightful feedback.

Let's think of this in an adult scenario. Let's say that you have always been interested in tennis, but never played a game. You decide to take some lessons. You, along with another 12 beginners, start your first class. Does the tennis pro lead the group to a classroom where she discusses and demonstrates how to play tennis for an hour? No!

Once you stretch and loosen up, you begin by practicing swinging the tennis racket with tennis balls. All of the adult students spread out on the court as the coach models the swing: "You want your feet shoulder width apart. If you are right-handed, pivot on your right foot. Step forward with your left. Pull the racket back and swing. Everybody now."

The instruction continues, "Pivot. Step. Pull back and swing. Again. Pivot. Step. Pull back and swing." Each of the novice tennis players are practicing their forehand with modeling from the pro. After a few minutes, everyone continues as she walks around and gives targeted feedback. When she sees multiple students who need the same correction, she provides feedback to the entire group at one time: "Don't forget to pivot your foot."

If the teacher spent 45 minutes of the first lesson providing instruction and modeling, then asked students to practice their swings without feedback, you would quit. It wouldn't make any sense. As teachers and educational leaders, we have to create classroom contexts in which students get tons of practice turns and feedback. Again, that is the first thing I look for during any classroom visit. At the end of the day, all learning boils down to practice turns and feedback.

There is something else that needs mentioning. As educators, we must have this tremendous urgency. Every second that we have with students is incredibly valuable. As leaders, we want to model that urgency. We must protect instructional time for our youngsters by protecting the time of teachers. We must use great caution when we assign additional duties to teachers that take away from their instructional planning, delivery, and assessment. In fact, wherever possible, we need to strip teachers of meaningless activities and responsibilities that eat up their time and cognitive energy. We need to treat them as professionals and give them as much time as needed to help their youngsters learn.

I know that we will never be able to take away every responsibility that is not related to instruction, but we can certainly prioritize and remove many of the things that monopolize teachers' time and compromise their quality of instruction.

Teachers also have an obligation for urgency. When students enter their classroom, they should be off to the races. Many students have a depressed number of practice turns and feedback because there is a slow lull in classrooms.

Unfortunately, it is not uncommon to see wasted time or this tremendously slow pace.

Work should be waiting for students when they enter the classroom. It can be engaging and challenging work. Students should come in and get moving. Teachers should create instructional activities that quickly engage students and rack up those practice turns and corresponding feedback. A teacher must demonstrate the conviction that every wasted minute is a minute during which students are not learning. Without great urgency and enthusiasm, students will never get enough practice turns and feedback.

Provide Explicit Instruction

In addition to drastically increasing practice turns and feedback, I think providing explicit instruction is another core element of specially designed instruction. Some talented students perform quite well with a constructivist approach to teaching. When given limited information, they are able to guide their own learning, draw accurate conclusions, synthesize information, and move their education forward with correct knowledge and skills.

Most students with disabilities and many other students, however, need explicit instruction to master many skills, processes, and academic competencies. Decades ago Anita Archer coined the phrase, "I do it. We do it. You do it," to beautifully describe explicit instruction (Archer, A.L. & Hughes, C.A., 2011). Most of our students with disabilities need clear modeling, guided practice, and then independent practice. Students need to see what it looks like, to attempt the skill or process with scaffolded support, and then attempt the skill independently.

At times, that arch of instruction will include many students over an entire class period, while at other times it will involve individual instruction to a student when he asks for help. "Let me show you how. Let's do it together. Now, you try it."

Unfortunately, explicit instruction has received an undeserved bad reputation as some consider it the opposite of rigor. This perception is false. A few years ago, I was installing wainscoting in my kitchen while possessing very few "handyman" skills. Fortunately, a neighbor who is a master carpenter worked with me as I learned to use the appropriate saws, measure for accuracy, and install (almost) seamless corners. He showed me how to do it. I tried it with his help. Then, I did it independently.

> **Explicit instruction is absolutely not synonymous with low rigor.**

After a few days, I was on my own and only called him when I needed some input. My neighbor, who had no training in pedagogy, provided explicit instruction. His guidance was not insulting, juvenile, nor did it lack rigor. He guided me through the steps that I needed to gain those skills. As special education leaders, we must work with our teachers so students are provided that same type of explicit, systematic instruction.

We see an example of explicit feedback, part of the explicit instruction cycle, when we watch incredible athletes, the best in the world in their respective sports. Watch the NFL, college football, the NBA, or Summer Olympic Games. When an athlete comes off of the floor or competition field, the coach provides explicit and direct feedback. When a guard misses a tackle and you see the coach yelling in the player's face mask, the coach certainly isn't saying, "What do you think you could do better?" No. He's giving the player an earful: "You didn't wrap the player and drive with your legs. You need to wrap and drive!" He is providing clear directions on what needs to be improved. (In our classrooms, we absolutely don't want to see the yelling component, but we certainly want to see our teachers providing explicit feedback.)

When an Olympic gymnast finishes the first vault and then prepares for her second, you see the coach providing clear directions. Most of the time, you even see the coach demonstrating with her body. Even if you can't hear her words, it is clear that the coach is providing explicit feedback: "Extend. Quick push off the vault."

These athletes are the best in the world. There are only a handful of individuals across the globe who are competing in their sport at a more rigorous level and yet, they are participating in explicit coaching and feedback. Therefore, explicit instruction should not be associated with low rigor. Explicit instruction is extremely beneficial for athletes at the top of their game, at the greatest levels of rigor, as well as for a wide variety of students, including, but certainly not limited to, students with disabilities.

Another point regarding explicit instruction is critical. For students with disabilities, and many other students, explicit instruction is needed not only in academic areas, but also in the areas of social skills, self-management, and vocational skills, among others. As special education leaders, we can assist school personnel in addressing all of these non-academic issues with highly systematic and explicit instruction.

Provide Effective Vocabulary Instruction

Is *effective* vocabulary instruction a fundamental element of both specially designed instruction and great universal instruction? I think so. Note the word "effective." Unfortunately, we see lots of ineffective vocabulary instruction in schools.

In many classrooms, we see students working on a list of vocabulary words that has been pulled from some website or supposedly from some expert's list. Unfortunately, that list is not connected to any curricular content. The student is learning the list of words and perhaps the definition, but really doesn't have much context to connect it to.

Sometimes, we see lists of terms that are connected to the curricular content, or words used across the various content areas, but the instructional activities are ineffective. Unfortunately, the vocabulary instruction includes writing the words, copying the definitions of the words, and then using them in a sentence. The terms might be appropriate and connected to the child's daily school work, but the instructional pedagogy is wanting.

What do we know about vocabulary and how it develops? Think of it as a web (or schema). When children learn about airplanes, and perhaps even have the experience of flying on a plane, through their experiences, conversations, and activities, they might learn about the different sizes and shapes of planes and their use. A large powerful passenger plane, such as a 747, is used to get lots of travelers from one location to another while a cargo plane has a different purpose.

Students might learn about airplane food, airports, delayed flight times, security checkpoints, military planes, air drag, the Wright brothers, air battles, etc., etc., etc. As children learn all of these ideas, they build deeper and deeper connections. The web or schema grows as more terms, experiences, and knowledge connect to other ideas and terminology. Now, in your head make that web a rotating 3-D model that has endless connections. Airplane food connects to all food. Air travel connects to other forms of travel. The idea of flight connects to bird migration, and so on and so on.

Vocabulary instruction is not about learning the dictionary definition of a list of different terms. Vocabulary instruction is about learning different concepts and how those concepts are related to a network of other concepts—a web or schema of connections. Vocabulary is about learning terms that represent very different yet interconnected concepts. It is expanding knowledge about those terms as you interact with those concepts. Vocabulary instruction is about developing this three dimensional, rotating fabric of language that represents concepts, connections, insights, experiences, and knowledge. Gradually, that fabric becomes thicker and more expansive as new concepts are added and existing concepts are deepened and strengthened.

In his book, *Building Background Knowledge for Academic Achievement*, Dr. Robert Marzano (2004) makes this point. A student's likelihood of success when learning new information depends on her background knowledge in a particular area of study. Background knowledge is someone's breadth and depth on a particular topic. The best way to determine a person's background knowledge of a topic is to determine their vocabulary related to the topic, whether it be art, algebra, or aardvarks. To extend that premise, in order to equip a person to be successful in a particular area of study, it is beneficial to build the person's vocabulary, or web of concepts, related to that topic and the terminology that represents all of the relevant concepts.

To take the air travel example a bit further, the student who is charged with learning about air transportation will be more successful incorporating new information if he already has a web of understanding in that general topic—a schema of background information—because he already has a network to which he can connect new terms and concepts. A student who has very limited background information, or schema, related to air travel, will be less astute at learning new information. His web is limited, so there are fewer points to which connections can be made. Therefore, if we are going to equip students to learn about air travel, we need to provide effective instruction, or build that student's background knowledge, so that he can be successful in learning additional information.

How does this approach impact students with disabilities? Certainly every student with a disability is different, but we can probably make some helpful generalized statements. If Cecelia has a specific learning disability, for example, then she has a processing problem which may impact how she pulls in information, processes that information, and then connects it to her knowledge schema or web.

Many students with disabilities have had the same experiences and instruction as their non-disabled peers, but they have been less astute at gathering new information formally through instruction, but also informally, through every day experiences and systematically "logging in" that information to make a coordinated schema or web of information. So, many students with disabilities have limited schemas or webs, or inefficient webs, which interfere with additional learning.

> Is *effective* vocabulary instruction a fundamental element of specially designed instruction (and actually great universal instruction)? I think so.

We have to provide both explicit and implicit vocabulary instruction for all students, but especially for those students who struggle or have difficulties. We must determine terminology that is both generalizable across content areas, or have high transferability, as well as those very specific content terms which systematically help students develop a fabric of understanding around those terms that grows and deepens and connects to other terms.

We have to provide students with an enormously rich language environment where there is excitement when new words are discovered in speaking, reading, and listening. We need to pull those words aside spontaneously and dig into their usage and meanings. Some educators might argue that students need implicit instruction (harvesting and digging into words when they are encountered) at the exclusion of explicit vocabulary instruction. The truth is, all students need both—explicit and implicit vocabulary instruction—and they also need tremendous exposure to new concepts, ideas, and the terminology that describes those things in language-rich environments.

To dig a little further into the explicit instruction, Marzano's book (2004) offers six steps to build students' vocabulary. The six steps include the following:

- *The teacher provides a description, explanation, or example of the term.*
- *Students restate the description, explanation, or example in their own words.*
- *Students construct a picture, pictograph, symbolic representation, or act out the term.*
- *The teacher extends and refines understanding of the word by engaging students in activities that help them add to their knowledge of the terms in vocabulary notebooks.*
- *Periodically ask students to discuss the terms with one another.*
- *Involve students in games that enable them to play with the terms and reinforce word knowledge.*

Implement Fill-the-Gap Interventions

Continuing to add to our list of specially designed instructional practices, let's look at fill-the-gap interventions. Several years ago, most students with disabilities were taught on their instructional level. If Billy was in the seventh grade, but read on the fourth-grade level, his reading instruction was also on the fourth-grade level. The materials that were used looked age appropriate, but he wasn't receiving instruction on his assigned grade in school. With this approach, the hope was that the students would "catch up." For many students, unfortunately, that did not happen.

That practice changed with the advent of the No Child Left Behind (NCLB) legislation (2001). With the new law, all students, including students with disabilities, were evaluated with assessments from their assigned grade and they were included in the accountability process. Eighth graders were evaluated with the eighth grade statewide assessments, third graders with the third-grade tests, and so on. As you would imagine, instructional patterns shifted. If students were going to be assessed on their assigned grade, then they needed instruction at that level. Across the country, students with disabilities started receiving instruction according to their assigned grade and many more students were educated in general education classes.

This change in instructional practices marked a huge step forward. Many students with disabilities were successful. Outstanding! This shift reflected a much better approach to educating students with disabilities. We saw some students meet higher expectations than were previously thought possible.

We have noticed, however, that some students with disabilities have holes in their learning that interfere with their ability to meet grade-assigned expectations. For many of us, our perspective has evolved. We now know that many students with disabilities need *both*. They need instruction on their assigned grade level and they also need fill-the-gap interventions.

Fortunately, students with disabilities are not the only students who have these dual needs. Many students who do not have disabilities participate in tiers of interventions *and* grade-assigned instruction. The Response to Intervention (RTI) or Multi-Tiered System of Supports (MTSS) approaches, whatever you call them in your school district, are implemented in order to assist non-disabled students and fill those holes.

Therefore, there are students who struggle, but are not identified as having disabilities who need this dual approach to instruction. In addition, there are students with disabilities who have qualified for services and they still need both—grade-assigned instruction and fill-the-gap interventions. Why can't all of those students receive those interventions (and certainly much of that instruction) at the same time and place if they have the same needs? Unfortunately, the RTI or MTSS processes in many, and perhaps most schools, are ineffective.

Let me offer one scenario that illustrates this problem. Let's pretend that you take your own child to the dentist for a routine cleaning. You wait in the lobby and read a magazine (or more likely complete some special education paper work). After a while, the dentist approaches to have a word with you, "Unfortunately, your child has a cavity. We are going to have a meeting to determine what we should do. There will be a few dental hygienists in the meeting. They will bring their best ideas, including some procedures they found online. I will be there to offer my thoughts, and we want you to attend as well. As a committee, we'll decide what to do next." As the parent in this scenario, what would you do? I know what I would do. I would run!

Does this sound similar to how interventions are provided in your school or district? Are the Response to Intervention processes or the Multi-Tiered System of Supports mechanisms implemented in a similar way? When students struggle or have gaps in their learning, are there way too many meetings, too much paper work, and ultimately very little impact for students?

Do educators in your schools think of RTI or MTSS as a series of meetings with tons of paper work but not truly as a way to impact students? Are the RTI and MTSS processes "the hoops to jump through" before you can refer a student for a special education evaluation? Do you hear, "How many weeks do we have to do this before Joshua gets a special education evaluation?" (For the purposes of this book, we are using RTI and MTSS synonymously even though there are some differences.)

You might wonder why this book includes references to RTI or MTSS when we are focusing on students with disabilities. There are two groups of students who need fill-the-gap interventions—general education students who are struggling and students with disabilities. Those interventions can occur at the same time during the school day as part of RTI or MTSS. Just because a student has already qualified for special education does not mean that he no longer has gaps in his learning or that he would not benefit from those interventions. Again, why can't students with disabilities participate in the interventions along with their non-disabled peers?

Let's return to the dentist analogy for a moment. Why, as I said before, would I snatch up my child and run from the office? A dentist should know how to fill a cavity. When Dr. Dentist wakes up in the morning, even before his feet hit the floor, he should already know that he will fill cavities that day. He will pull some teeth and his dental hygienists will spend much of their day on routine cleanings. For dentists, such procedures are automatic. They should be ready to go when their patients need them.

Before they open their office doors in the morning, they might not know which patients will need specific procedures, but they know that someone will need them. Again, routine stuff. If an exam indicated that a child did, in fact, need something less routine and more complex, then a referral or some additional research might be in order. For typical procedures, however, the dentist and his staff should be ready to go.

In our schools, we need to be equally prepared to provide interventions for those common needs and typical holes in learning. We see different students with similar weaknesses year after year. In virtually every high school across the country, for example, some students enter ninth grade with challenges in mathematics. Sometimes such students are few in number; at other times, their numbers are far greater. Every year, the math teachers say, "This year, some of my students can't even _____." Fill in the blank.

What do many high schools do when faced with these ninth-grade students? Unfortunately, Ms. Wyatt, the math teacher on this side of the hall, tries her best to meet the needs of her students. Mr. Jones, the math teacher on the other side of the hall, helps his students the best way he can. Dr. Johnson in the next room tries his best to find solutions as well. Even though we experience this scenario year after year at many high schools, we treat it like a surprise. Does this sound efficient or effective?

If we absolutely know that some ninth-grade students are going to lack some prerequisite skills in math, then we should prepare in advance for those students. We should have interventions already in place. While we might not know who those youngsters will be, we are fairly certain *somebody* will display deficiencies in mathematics, so we should have interventions ready and waiting.

In fact, in many cases, we *do* know who those students will be. If a student has been enrolled in your school district, even if they were not in your specific school, then you have tons of data on that child. Depending on how long he has been in the district, you might have multiple years of achievement information, attendance data, health records, behavioral histories, and so on. You know which students will struggle in mathematics in your high school before they cross the threshold for the first time. The data, along with some additional information (perhaps from a diagnostic assessment), will determine the specific holes in learning that should be addressed.

This scenario is not limited to high schools. We see common holes in learning at all grade levels. You have fourth graders, for example, who have difficulty with oral reading fluency. You might have third graders who have trouble with the conceptual underpinning of a mathematical principle. Some students have a history of behavioral issues while others routinely miss school.

Similar to the dentist analogy above, how we often implement RTI or MTSS is just as inefficient. When a student has academic holes in learning, behavioral challenges, or attendance issues, we often call a meeting with the parents and others and act like it is the first time we have seen a youngster with these needs. We brainstorm from scratch and fill out lots of paperwork. Our valuable and precious time is being spent in meetings and discussions rather than helping youngsters.

We need standard intervention protocols ready and waiting for students who have common holes in learning. When a student's oral reading fluency skills are a couple of years behind, then we need a handful of research-based interventions that can be considered for the student ready and waiting at the school.

Each school does not need an endless list of interventions for oral reading fluency, nor does every teacher need to search a wide variety of solutions on the internet, where one is as likely to find ineffective solutions as they are to find effective ones.

Before the school year even starts, the school needs to determine the 8-12 common holes in learning and select a few research or evidenced-based interventions for those common needs. While they are at it, they need to select validated progress monitoring tools that they will implement for each of those holes in learning.

After selecting these standard intervention protocols, the faculty needs to be trained in their delivery. In fact, the faculty members can be critical partners in choosing the menu of research-based interventions. With this limited but pragmatic scope of interventions, as well as the pre-established validated progress monitoring tools, teachers and paraprofessionals can be trained deeply in the delivery of those interventions and receive ongoing coaching.

Teachers will feel confident in their ability to identify students with areas of need and will more likely trigger effective interventions if the interventions and measurement tools are already in place. Instead of starting from scratch, like in the dentist analogy, schools are prepared for students and the various needs that we know some of them will bring. This ready-to-go menu can fall under three umbrella categories: academic skills, behavioral needs, and attendance issues.

Above, I mentioned standard intervention protocols. The truth is that there are two different philosophical approaches to implementing RTI or MTSS: the use of standard intervention protocols or the problem-solving approach.

The standard intervention protocol approach has basically been described above. The problem-solving approach, with the risk of oversimplifying, focuses on problem solving for each youngster who indicates a need. The truth is, we need to combine both approaches into a hybrid approach.

> There are two groups of students who need fill-the-gap interventions— general education students who are struggling and students with disabilities. Those interventions can occur at the same time during the school day as part of RTI or MTSS. Just because a student has already qualified for special education does not mean that he no longer has gaps in his learning or that he would not benefit from those interventions.

Even though you should have standard intervention protocols ready and waiting for students, problem solving should be embedded throughout the process. You should not have only one intervention for each area of need. There should be a menu, albeit a manageable menu of interventions, for each weakness. The student's teachers should consider the needs and history of the student before determining which of the interventions on the menu should be attempted first for the student.

In elementary school, and perhaps middle school, RTI or MTSS usually focuses on specific, discreet skills that need addressing. One would not develop an intervention for "reading" in general; one needs to determine which of the five dimensions of reading should be improved and which specific skills under the specific domain need developing. The more adept a school is at identifying the specific and detailed hole in learning, the more impactful the aligned intervention can actually be.

Working under this scenario, communications with parents become more tailored and more purposeful: "Ms. Smith, we are so lucky to have Felicia in our fifth-grade class. We have noticed that she has some difficulties with reading comprehension. As we looked more closely at her abilities, we found that she has some underlying deficits in phonics skills. When she sees a word she doesn't know, she has some difficulties with the letter-sound relationships necessary to decode the word. Have you seen Felicia struggle in a similar way?"... "We analyzed her skills and noticed that she decodes simple words easily, but has trouble with decoding multi-syllabic words—those words that have more than one syllable. We have a number of youngsters who have this weakness and we already have interventions in place to address her particular need. For Felicia, we are going to implement a specific intervention called..." This kind of conversation can occur over the phone or at a regularly scheduled parent-teacher conference.

Doesn't that conversation sound so much more prepared than many conversations with parents regarding the need for RTI or MTSS? An RTI or MTSS meeting with the parent is not even necessary for routine needs. (You should always keep the parent informed through a phone call or during a routine parent-teacher conference.) If a few interventions are attempted and the data indicate a lack of sufficient progress, then calling a meeting with Ms. Smith and other professionals becomes necessary in order to dig a little deeper, to analyze the area of weakness more closely, and to choose the best intervention methods. As always, you need to follow your state's requirements regarding when parent consent is needed for analyzing student needs.

The Georgia Pyramid of Interventions (2011) has four tiers, which is very unusual across the country. Most states' RTI or MTSS models have a total of 3 tiers. The Georgia model includes universal or core instruction (Tier 1) and specially designed instruction (special education) at Tier 4. The fill-the-gap interventions are separated into Tier 2 and Tier 3.

Tier 3 includes and is synonymous with the Student Support Team (SST). For roughly 30 years, it has been a state requirement that every school has a team that brainstorms the needs and next steps when a child is struggling. The meeting must include select school personnel, and the parents must be invited.

This team at each school was initially instituted and required in the 1980s to curb the tide of inappropriate referrals to special education. The hope was that by having a committee that brainstormed the needs of struggling students, more children would be successful in general education and the initial reaction to refer a student for a special education evaluation would be reduced.

Tier 2 is the place where schools implement these automatic interventions (*without* process-heavy meetings). In the Henry County School System in Georgia, for example, tremendous work has been done to assist schools in the development of "go to" menus that detail common areas of need along with aligned Research-based

Interventions and Validated Progress Monitoring Tools. With these menus in place, schools are prepared for common holes in learning.

If students do not display sufficient progress at Tier 2, then the child is referred to Tier 3, which includes the Student Support Team, where the parents and a team of professionals can brainstorm further to select different interventions. Ultimately, if students prove unsuccessful with Tier 3 interventions, based on the ongoing analysis of the data and a disability is expected, then a referral for a special education evaluation can occur.

The discussion of a four-tier RTI or MTSS model may sound bothersome if you are in the majority of states that use a three-tier model. But it should not be. The only reason that I mention it is because Georgia's model provides an explicit separation between where automatic tiers can be launched (Tier 2) and where a little further analysis and brainstorming with the parents are needed.

If your state has a three-tier RTI or MTSS model, then you probably have that option also. At some level, the automatic interventions can be implemented without a formal meeting with the parent. When the student does not learn sufficiently with those interventions in place, then a meeting with the parents and other professionals are likely the next step. Again, even when the automatic interventions are implemented, ongoing communication with the parent is important. I would certainly want to know if the school thought that my child had some holes in learning. Knowing that the school already had standard interventions in place would only bolster my confidence in the school.

As students get older, especially in high schools, RTI or MTSS processes shift. A school does not necessarily focus *exclusively* on discreet academic holes in learning. If you want to see a bunch of blank faces, tell a group of high school teachers that they need to address a student's weaknesses in phonics skills. You will see eyes roll back, and you will not get any traction. Most high school teachers are not equipped for that work, nor should they be.

The ultimate goal for high schools is to enable students to earn their high school diploma and to be prepared for post-secondary education or the work force. High school personnel are completely focused on enabling students to master skills in a course and then earn Carnegie credits toward that diploma. Most high school teachers have significant expertise in their content area and the courses they teach and focus on delivering that instruction.

As mentioned earlier, some students enter high school with holes in their prerequisite skills that will make passing their high school courses very difficult. To continue the conversation about math, some students don't have one or two specific holes in learning, their knowledge is littered with gaps.

In those circumstances, when students have significant difficulties in mathematics, reading, or written expression, they need entire courses in those content areas in order to shore up their entire knowledge base. Effective high schools identify those students who need a foundational math or English/language arts course and then schedule those students into the course. In many cases, the students can earn elective credit for participating in that course, thereby moving toward the ultimate goal of graduating with their peers and being college or career ready.

Even though a variety of students might be placed in a foundational English/language arts or math course in high school, they will not all have the same holes in learning and therefore should not follow the same sequence of interventions. As part of the course, the teacher should provide a diagnostic assessment which will pinpoint the exact skills that need addressing.

In addition to missing prerequisite skills, there are a variety of other reasons why students have difficulty being successful in high school. In some cases, students have low grades because they have not submitted several assignments. If that is the case, the school has to determine the reason why each student is missing assignments. Is it because she does not have the knowledge to turn in the work? Is it because she does not have the discipline or school work is not a priority? Or, is it because the student has problems with organizational skills?

For each of these causes, the supportive actions will look different. Just as you must match an intervention to a specific area of weakness, the support actions, though perhaps not technically interventions, must match each student's needs. If a student has the prerequisite skills to learn the content in the class, but is having trouble understanding the content and therefore not submitting assignments, then the student needs additional instruction in the content area.

If the student does not prioritize school work and is not committed to completing the assignments, but has the understanding to do so, then perhaps she needs to participate in supervised work time in which the assignments can be completed under the watchful eye of supportive adults. This can also be a scenario in which a strong partnership with the family might be helpful.

When students fail to submit assignments, the core reason must be determined so that appropriate next steps can be taken. In addition, there are other reasons why students have difficulty in high school. Some students have difficulty making connections with peers and adults. This might lead to student absences and an ultimate disregard for the importance of education. The transition to high school can be very difficult for students who lack the ability to make connections. For these youngsters, supportive actions might include establishing peer and/or adult mentorships and ensuring that students are connected to classes or extra-curricular activities that are engaging and meaningful for the student. There has to be a connection, with people and activities, developed for the youngsters.

In order for high school RTI or MTSS processes to be successful, schools must be ready with the variety of actions noted above: courses that provide foundational skills in the areas of mathematics and English/language arts, additional instruction in the core courses for students who have trouble mastering the content, additional support systems to help students complete assignments, organizational techniques that assist students who are lacking in those skills (something that will be addressed more fully in the next session), and specific activities to help engage and connect students to the high school community.

Just like RTI or MTSS at the elementary or middle-school level, the key is matching the interventions or supportive activity to the specific area of weakness for each student. In addition, school personnel must be self-reflective when the universal instruction must be improved to equip more students to be successful without additional tiers of supports. As noted earlier, effective tiers of interventions or fantastic specially designed instruction, no matter how powerful, can never make up for ineffective universal instruction.

Again, just like elementary or middle schools, there are students with disabilities who need these supports as well as many other students who require this assistance. In the overwhelming majority of cases, both students with disabilities and their peers who do not have disabilities can participate in the activities at the same time.

In this section, I have only touched the surface of building an effective RTI or MTSS system. I certainly have not done it justice. In fact, RTI or MTSS is really a school improvement framework that involves improving all the core instruction, interventions, and the specially designed instruction provided in a school. For our purposes, I have limited the discussion to the intervention components.

The whole purpose of this section is to clarify that many students with disabilities not only need interventions in addition to effective grade-level instruction, but they also need specially designed instruction, none of which can be left up to the creativity, enthusiasm, or diligence of any individual teacher. Every school must have in place a systematic procedure that, when necessary, triggers interventions that meet the students' unique academic, behavioral, or attendance needs.

Provide Metacognitive Instruction

Metacognition is often referred to as thinking about thinking. It can also be understood as the self-awareness of how one approaches a problem or a task. For example, if LaTonya is asked to write a persuasive essay on a topic of her choice when given 15 topics to choose from, she has to make a plan. LaTonya might include these among her list of steps:

- Reviewing the topics and eliminating all topics that do not interest her.
- Choosing three topics that interest her the most.
- Listing everything she knows about each of those three topics.
- Choosing the topic that she prefers after reviewing her lists.

Once LaTonya decides on a particular topic, then she has to make another plan that will lead to her finished product. These steps might include the following:

- Developing a word web that organizes her argument in defense of her position.
- Drafting a position statement for the overall paper and a topic sentence for each paragraph.
- Developing a hook for the introductory paragraph that leads to her position statement.

- Composing a working draft of her entire paper.
- Reviewing her draft against the rubric provided by the teacher.
- Asking a fellow student to review the draft and to make suggestions.
- Revising the draft to better meet the expectations outlined on the rubric.
- Developing a final, polished draft that she can submit to her teacher.

This seems somewhat complicated when you list the steps, but every English teacher is accustomed to these steps, even if they refer to them with different terminology. In addition, most English teachers provide instruction on the various steps, and they provide ongoing assessment and feedback to students as they complete each step along the way.

Metacognition involves the ability to develop a plan for a multi-day project like the essay outlined above, but it also involves a wide variety of tasks that people perform every day. It includes the ability to self-analyze a situation that just occurred and learn from that situation.

For example, some students with disabilities have difficulty with social situations. Let's say Leonard is in a social situation in which everyone is very serious. Perhaps his friends are discussing Ms. Freeman, their classroom teacher, who is absent from school because of an unexpected hospitalization. Leonard might make an inappropriate joke, not because he is insensitive but because he has difficulty with certain social situations. He might not grasp why his friends give him awkward looks after his joke.

Leonard does not have the self-awareness or metacognition to process the situation. An effective teacher will teach Leonard that, in general, cracking a joke is not the best idea when other people appear serious. He has to be taught how to analyze situations and how to make decisions about how best to move forward.

Some might argue that the scenario above falls more under social skills training instead of metacognition, and that's fine. The point is that many students with disabilities have significant deficits in self-awareness about how to approach, think about, and organize their actions in a wide variety of situations and how to learn from past experiences.

Some students lack the ability to manage taking multiple classes from multiple teachers. They have difficulty prioritizing their activities, understanding the different temperaments of teachers, breaking tasks into steps, and so on. They lack the ability to make the most strategic next step to be successful in the different teachers' classes.

You also see a weakness in metacognitive skills when a student opens his locker and piles of books and papers fall out or when a student takes a multiple-choice test and does not know how to eliminate obviously incorrect answers. Some students write their homework assignment on a piece of paper but misplace the paper by the time they arrive home, or they remember the paper but cannot make sense of what they wrote five hours earlier.

I propose that specially designed instruction should include explicit instruction regarding metacognition. We must systematically help students think about how to approach, organize, and plan their work. We must teach them how to be self-reflective about situations to determine what they could have done more effectively in that context.

This process should begin when the teacher provides the steps students should accomplish toward finishing an activity, project, or assignment. For example, many students with *and without* disabilities should be provided with an electronic or hard copy planner and ongoing instruction and feedback about how to use it. The teacher should write the homework assignment on the board and should instruct every student to copy the assignment. Then the teacher should ensure that every student in the class has placed that written assignment in the homework folder in their planner. Each step needs directions and feedback from the teacher. Another folder should house documents that need to go home for their parents and so on.

Many schools provide planners for students, but then leave the use of those planners up to the students when they need more support than that. As students grow older, especially in high school, teachers and administrators often say, "Our students must take responsibility to do that." We certainly do want to build responsibility in our students, especially as they get older, but if a student does not have the skills to do what is expected, then that student needs instruction and support.

In recent years, another element of metacognition has received a lot of press. It is very beneficial for students to set goals, develop action steps to meet those goals, and reflect on their progress. This process is good for all students. Just like any other metacognitive process, some students will need instruction on how to set goals and how to develop action steps to move toward those goals. They will then need instruction on how to reflect on their progress and how to revise action steps as needed.

> Specially designed instruction should include explicit instruction regarding metacognition. We must systematically help students think about how to approach, organize, and plan their work. We must teach them how to be self-reflective about situations to determine what they could have done more effectively in that context.

As with all explicit instruction, metacognitive instruction must include teacher demonstration or modeling and guided practice while the students make attempts with support. Over time, the support provided is lessened as students become accurate with the task. Eventually, the support is removed so students can complete the task independently. This process of metacognitive instruction must be intentional and specific. Ideally, the same approach should be used across teachers, whether the students are using a planner, reading informational text, completing a multi-week project, or completing written assignments. That consistency will establish common expectations and increase practice turns for the students.

It should be noted that metacognitive instruction is really required for all students at different points and ages in their learning. Even as students grow older, many non-disabled students will need this type of instruction. It is not uncommon at all for students to reach the sixth week of their freshman year in high school and realize that they have very weak grades. Some high school teachers will say that some students do not take their high school courses seriously until their first round of grades are posted. Some of that is certainly true. But many students, including students with and without disabilities, do not have the metacognitive skills to be successful with the increased demands of high school.

In this chapter, we have reviewed five of the six instructional practices that I think should create the foundation for specially designed instruction. Building an effective behavioral system, the last practice on my list, is covered in the next chapter.

Again, my desire is not that each and every school and school district adopt my list. My goal is to encourage each and every school and school district to have a list of its own. Furthermore, we cannot expect our teachers to implement specially designed instruction if we do not provide some guidance, training, and support to help them do so.

Guiding Questions

- Across your school district, have you defined specific instructional practices that should be implemented as the foundation for students with disabilities? If not, what practices should be on your district's list?

- In your school district, are there priority instructional practices that are being implemented by the curriculum and instruction department? Which of those priority practices can be enlarged to have a significant impact on the achievement of students with disabilities?

V
Effective Behavioral Systems

The last recommended instructional practice that can be implemented in all content-area classes, and for that matter across the entire school, is effective behavioral systems. There are many facets and components to implementing this instructional practice, so it gets its own chapter. Many books have been published on this topic alone, so I certainly won't do it justice, but I'll hit some highlights. Let's start with a few main principles regarding behavior.

Students Must Be Taught Behavioral Skills

When a student enters first grade, we know that she will need instruction in order to learn to read. Deidra's teacher systematically plans and implements instruction to take Deidra from her current skill level to mastery of the first grade reading standards by the end of the school year.

During her lessons, Deidra participates in instruction and works on her new skills. She also receives feedback on her attempts. When she completes the work accurately, Ms. James reinforces her efforts, "You read that so nicely. I like how you read so smoothly." When Deidra makes mistakes, Ms. James provides further instruction and feedback, "Let's read that word again. What does the letter 'a' say in this word?"

At every grade, we assume that students need instruction in order to master grade-level standards. We know that students will enter the grade with some skills, but as educators we know our job is to provide instructional experiences and ongoing support so students' skills and competencies are improved.

We should approach behavioral skills in the same way. When students enter the school year, there should be a plan in place for teaching them the appropriate way to interact with one another, teachers, and any other adults encountered in the school environment. We should provide systematic instruction.

We certainly see this in kindergarten and many elementary school classes. The teachers show students how to line up in the hallway, how to transition between activities in the class, how to raise their hand to be called on, and so on. When students perform those skills with accuracy, fantastic teachers provide encouragement: "Class, I am so proud of you. Everyone is lined up on the second tile." When students need correction, outstanding teachers find a wide variety of ways to provide correction: "I'm looking to see who is lined up on the second tile."

As students get older, we see this type of behavioral instruction less and less. At the beginning of the school year, most teachers at different instructional levels review the expectations and tell students the class or school rules. In some classes, that information is limited to summarizing the district's code of conduct. No other behavior instruction (if you can even be lenient and call that instruction) is provided.

Would that ever work for the teaching of reading, mathematics, or biology? Would it ever be appropriate to merely list the skills that need to be mastered during the year and call it done? Of course not.

Students need instruction in their subjects every day in order to build competency in those subjects. Likewise, students need instruction, feedback, and support regarding their behavior. That does not mean that every teacher must set aside 15 minutes in every class to teach behavioral skills, but systematic instruction and modelling should be provided frequently.

> When students enter the school year, there should be a plan in place for teaching them the appropriate way to interact with one another, teachers, and any other adults encountered in the school environment. We should provide systematic instruction.

In addition, teachers should provide ongoing encouragement and reinforcement if we want students to continue to show us the behaviors we want to see. Similarly, teachers should provide effective feedback when youngsters step outside of what is expected. The delivery of encouragement and corrective feedback should be intentional and specific in order to be effective.

At the end of the day, we have to focus on teaching children how they should conduct themselves—what appropriate and responsible behavior looks like. Such a deliberate approach is so much more productive and impactful than only focusing on ending the negative behavior.

With the implementation of positive behavior interventions and supports (PBIS) across the country, we see much more instruction, encouragement, and effective redirection provided for students regarding behavior. That is a good thing. Our knowledge of school-wide behavioral systems has increased with the implementation of PBIS, especially when it is implemented with fidelity.

Behavior Is Communication

If you are fortunate enough to be a parent, I bet you can remember those early days. You came home from the hospital with your newborn. When you put your infant son or daughter down for a nap, you listened closely. What did you do when she cried? You picked her up. She continued to cry. You changed her diaper. Still cried. You fed her and she stopped crying. When your baby daughter was just a few days old, you realized that her behavior was communicating a need to you. When your baby cried, you did your best to determine what your baby needed in order to stop crying (O'Connor, 1998).

All behavior, both positive and negative, can be thought of as a form of communication. That does not mean that all people in all circumstances intend for their behaviors to be interpreted as a form of communication, but behavior does, nonetheless, communicate something. We instinctively respond to our infants' cries in order to respond to their needs.

Unfortunately, we often forget that principle of communication when students get older and their behavior becomes less cute and adorable. When students (and really humans of all ages) display any type of behavior, there is communication in that behavior, even if unintentional. When you observe a student fully engaged in his work, there is communication. When a student ignores a request, there is communication. When a student avoids his work, there is communication. One of the first steps in being more effective at promoting positive student behaviors is realizing that their behavior is communicative. As educators in the school setting, our job is to be insightful in determining the underlying message communicated by student behavior.

Behavior Has a Purpose

Virtually all observable behaviors serve a purpose. As adults, we wear certain clothes because they serve a purpose. The clothes might be highly functional for jobs, such as a doctor's scrubs or a construction worker's hard hat. Some clothes might serve an aesthetic purpose. We might prefer how we look in certain fabrics, sizes, and styles. Some clothes feel comfortable. Whatever the reason, the clothes we choose to purchase and to wear serve a purpose.

That same principle applies to all behaviors. You greet people a certain way because it has become effective for you. You choose certain phrases and body movements because they work for you. That does not mean that you have explicitly evaluated every action you take when you greet someone, or any of the thousands of tiny behaviors you perform on a daily basis, but you have learned that certain behaviors work for you, even if unconsciously, so you continue to do them. They serve their purpose.

Sometimes, we even see adults who exhibit behaviors that are self-destructive, and we naturally wonder why someone would continue such behaviors. Take addictive behavior, for example. Why would someone spend an enormous amount of time and money on illegal drugs, and possibly do harm to themselves and to their family and friends? Because even self-destructive, addictive behaviors serve a purpose. The addict might be medicating some type of emotional pain or psychological discomfort. Those behaviors serve an immediate need even if there are negative long-term or short-term consequences. The adults may not be able to describe why they perform certain behaviors, but they would not continue to do so unless the behaviors served a purpose.

In one of my previous jobs, I worked with an individual who dominated every meeting and conversation. Regardless of the topic of the discussion or the purpose of the meeting, she always spoke the most. After a while, I noticed that other professionals rarely voiced any opinions when she was in the room. They spoke very little or not at all. My talkative colleague's behavior served her purpose—even if subconsciously. She learned that when she dominated the conversation or meeting, she encountered very little resistance and was not limited by the recommendations of others. Her initiatives progressed in the direction she intended them to. She did not have to alter her practices. By dominating the conversation, she accomplished a purpose.

As special education administrators, we understand that all behaviors, both good and bad, serve a purpose. That is why functional behavioral assessments are conducted. We collect and objectively analyze data to determine the function of a negative behavior. We determine what patterns are present, what antecedents typically occur, and what reinforcers are set in motion following the misbehavior. Then we try to alter the experiences of the child so that he can get what he is seeking with more appropriate behavior. As special education administrators, that perspective is well known. As leaders, our job is to help other professionals see the connection between behavior and purpose.

Student Behavior Improves with Engaging Instruction

Students with disabilities need GREAT instruction. The "E" in the acronym reminds us that instruction must be engaging and exciting. It is impossible, and counterproductive, to discuss building behavioral systems without discussing instruction.

Our students spend seven or eight hours in school each day. We want instruction to enthrall their curiosity and pull them into the activities. We want the days to move by quickly for students because their activities are fun and exciting. We want to challenge and inspire our students. If we provide that type of instruction that sparks such engagement, many of the behavioral challenges that we see will be minimized. If a particular school has an issue with widespread negative student behavior throughout the school day, observe the classrooms. If you find the instruction listless, dull, and formulaic, you will need to address it.

Positive, Proactive Behavioral Systems

With these fundamental principles of behavior as our guide, we want school leaders and teachers to develop proactive and positive behavioral systems across their school and in their classrooms. Those systems will include defining what behaviors are expected and then determining what those expected behaviors actually look like. It also includes building trustful and respectful relationships between adults and students, and intentionally and explicitly teaching youngsters how to demonstrate those behaviors while at school. Those expected behaviors will include predictable rituals and routines as well as those soft skills that are so important.

Students with disabilities, and really all students, benefit from a solid school engagement and behavioral plan where students' positive behaviors are systematically grown just as we help youngsters develop their academic skills.

As special education leaders, we often get phone calls from school administrators who have concerns about a youngster's extremely negative behaviors.

We are certainly adept at helping principals respond to negative behaviors and providing immediate support. We are used to doing that. Our larger goal will be to help schools and teachers build proactive systems where positive behaviors are fostered and developed. That does not mean that we will still not have youngsters who have very significant emotional issues that result in extremely negative behaviors, but building proactive systems will create a foundation for better behavior from the overwhelming majority of our students.

Consequences

Now that we have addressed the need to establish positive and proactive behavioral systems, let us jump ahead to the discussion about consequences. As a special education administrator, I am sure that you spend much of your time helping schools negotiate various consequences for excessive misbehaviors. For our purposes today, let's set our focus on in-school and out-of-school suspensions. Since so many of our students receive suspensions, there are specific federal guidelines regarding the maximum number of days a student with a disability can be suspended out-of-school without providing instructional services.

First, let us ask an important question. Are suspensions effective? Well, whether or not we consider suspensions effective depends on our intended goal for suspending a student. The next logical question is: What is our intended goal for suspending a student? When posed this question, educators often chuckle because there are two answers: the truthful answer and the "professional" answer. The real answer is that suspensions serve many purposes: They "send a message to the parents," "show the student who is boss," or "give the teacher a break."

Unfortunately, those should not be the intended goals for suspending a student, or for any consequence for that matter. The purpose of any consequence, including suspensions, should be to reduce the chance that the negative behavior occurs again. Ideally, a consequence should also increase the likelihood that the student will adopt a positive replacement behavior.

Are suspensions effective at reducing negative behavior? Perhaps not. If suspensions reduced negative behavior, the school with the highest rates of suspensions this year would have the lowest rate of suspensions next year.

That is worth repeating. If suspensions reduced students' negative misbehavior, the school with the highest rate of suspensions this school year would have the lowest rate of suspensions next year. All of those suspensions would have improved the students' troubling behavior, and future suspensions would become far less frequent. Unfortunately, that is usually not the case. Schools that have high rates of suspension typically continue that pattern year after year. In general, the suspensions don't improve student behavior.

I am not making light of disciplinary infractions. Principals and other school personnel have a tremendous responsibility for keeping students safe. Unfortunately, headlines show us that some students across the country have made terrible and dangerous decisions. If you want to keep yourself up at night, consider the responsibility of keeping all students safe in a high school filled with hormone-fueled adolescents. That is a tremendous responsibility. Right now, let us only consider those misbehaviors that are bothersome, but not dangerous.

Back to the question, are suspensions reducing negative behaviors? For a small selection of students, perhaps. Most high school personnel will agree that suspensions might work for those individual students who are usually performing well academically and conducting themselves as model students. When those students misbehave and are assigned a suspension, they are extremely upset, as are their parents. Tears are shed in the principal's office. In that case, such suspensions might actually reduce the likelihood that the student repeats the negative misbehavior. That single suspension might have an impact on that particular student.

> If suspensions reduced students' negative misbehavior, the school with the highest rate of suspensions this school year would have the lowest rate of suspensions next year.

Unfortunately, that is not who we are suspending. Some students are stuck in a routine of repeated suspensions. They misbehave, get referred to the office, and then are assigned a suspension. In a few days, they return to school and the pattern repeats itself. In that case, suspensions do not seem to be curbing misbehavior.

In some cases, suspensions are actually *increasing* negative behavior. Instead of decreasing the student's unwanted behavior, the suspension actually increases the possibility that the student will commit the misbehavior again. In your school or district, are students suspended for skipping class or being tardy? Does that make any sense? In those instances, students do not want to go to class. Therefore, the consequence is to remove them from class. Students are receiving what they want. Their misbehavior of skipping class is being reinforced. Their negative behavior of habitually skipping class and receiving a suspension is serving their purpose of avoiding class.

Alternatives to Suspensions

What should we do when students misbehave? We need to implement consequences that actually reduce the chance that the negative behavior is repeated. In fact, our charge is greater than that. We not only want the students to reduce the negative behavior, we want them to replace that negative behavior with an appropriate, positive behavior. With that goal in mind, it might be beneficial to implement the following steps whenever a student is referred to the office.

- **Debrief the situation with the student:** An adult should discuss the misbehavior with the student and discuss why his actions were inappropriate. This is an opportunity to ensure that the student understands why what he did was unacceptable.

- **Make it right:** The student should then correct the situation. Depending on the age or developmental level of the student and the situation, this step might include one of the following:
  - ■ Making a verbal apology to the offended adult.
  - ■ Making a verbal apology and shaking hands with any offended student.
  - ■ Writing an apology that includes a promise of how the student will behave in the future. Younger students might draw a picture.
  - ■ Cleaning up at least a portion of any mess that was made. This should be implemented in accordance with the developmental level of the student. It is usually best if students don't use cleaning chemicals.
  - ■ Completing any missed assignments, which resulted from disrupted class time.
  - ■ It may be appropriate for the student to choose how he or she will "make it right."

- **Provide instruction on the desired behavior:** The adult should then provide clear and specific instruction on what the preferred, replacement behavior looks like. The adult should model this behavior, and the student should practice this behavior with feedback. (Before the direct instruction begins, it is appropriate to ask the student to demonstrate what he or she thinks would be an appropriate behavior. The demonstration will provide meaningful information to the adult to determine how much instruction is needed.) For elementary school students, this step is complete. For high school students, it is also appropriate that the student complete a written assignment that digs deeper into making better choices. For example, if Brian was disrespectful to an adult, then he can write a description of how his grandmother would have acted in that situation. Or, he could compare his behavior to the actions of various role models in history.

- **Demonstration of the desired behavior:** The adult should ask the student to demonstrate the expected behavior for a certain number of times over the next few days. When the student's teachers witness the student demonstrating the desired, replacement behavior (or an approximation of the behavior), then they sign the student's agreement. The teacher should verbally praise the student for making attempts at the desired behavior. An example of a documentation sheet is provided on the following page. It can be aged up or aged down depending on the developmental level of the student. The teacher should use this as an encouraging process to foster the new behavior. After the trial period (typically a few days), the student returns the paper to the school administrator who conducted the steps outlined on this page. The administrator should verbally reinforce the desired behavior.

Notice that we want to encourage the new, replacement behavior. There's an educational advice that says "what occurs immediately after a behavior will tell you if the behavior will reoccur." If we want the student to adopt the more positive behavior, we have to encourage and reinforce that behavior.

If the adult holds a grudge and pairs the signature with griping or rehashing the negative behavior, the student will likely not adopt the positive behavior. We want the adult to express gratitude and encouragement to the student for making better choices. We certainly want this new behavior to be repeated!

To be honest, if you want to shift the culture and climate in a school, which includes but is not limited to student behavior, then you must build a respectful and positive environment where proactive activities are implemented to shape students' behavior before negative behavior occurs. But when principals and assistant principals are asked to reduce their use of suspensions as disciplinary tools, their first response is, "What should I do when students misbehave?" As a leader, you must offer alternatives to suspensions, while recognizing that the long-term goal is to build a proactive school culture based on the principles of behavior.

_____ School

Student: _____

Over the next 2 days, I will _____
(desired behavior) at least 5 times.

Teachers, please sign this form
when you see _____
demonstrate the behavior described above.

1st Time _____ (Excellent!)

2nd Time _____ (Outstanding!)

3rd Time _____ (Thank You!)

4th Time _____ (Appreciate your effort!)

5th Time _____ (You met your goal!)

Please return this to
Mr./Mrs. _____
(administrator who assigned this form)
on _____ (date).

Suspension Disproportionality

We need to address another issue regarding suspensions. It is very clear that in the United States some racial and ethnic groups of students with disabilities are over-suspended for disciplinary reasons. African American students with disabilities across the country, for example, have a much higher risk of being suspended than students from other racial and ethnic groups. The 2004 Individuals with Disabilities Education Improvement Act (IDEIA) addresses this issue by requiring state departments of education to identify school districts that have significant racial disproportionality in their suspension practices for students with disabilities. Those identified school districts must correct their practices, including spending 15% of their IDEIA funds to remedy the discrepancy.

Whether the issue is addressed in the legislation or not, the over-suspension of various racial groups is a tragedy that we must address. This issue is extremely complicated. Unfortunately, I am not offering a clear set of solutions. Even though much has been published about suspension disproportionality (the clear evidence that it exists, potential causes, and theoretical solutions) a clear path for improvement has not been established.

There are many opinions and opinion-based articles available, but there is very little replicable research on how to correct the issue. In the absence of universally accepted researched-based solutions, I am offering some questions and ideas that might prove helpful as you engage your district in this extremely important and valuable work.

Is suspension disproportionality a "disability" issue?

No. The 2004 IDEIA federal legislation addresses suspension disproportionality exclusively for students with disabilities. The truth is that the over-suspension of some students with disabilities is merely a symptom of a larger problem. School districts are not merely over-suspending some minority students with disabilities. They are also over-suspending select minority students who do not have disabilities.

We cannot correct disproportionality for students with disabilities in isolation. In fact, because we know that disproportionality impacts non-disabled students, we have the moral obligation to address it for all students even if IDEIA only speaks to the disproportionality among students with disabilities. By addressing the larger issue for all students, we will, in turn, impact suspension rates for students with disabilities. Therefore, analyze the suspension patterns for all students of all races and ethnicities, and share that information with your district leaders. By bringing any discrepancy to the attention of district leaders, momentum will be garnered so that interventions are not driven by the special education department in your district.

Addressing suspension disproportionality for all students cannot be seen as a special education issue. It must be addressed by all educators. The special education department can certainly play a part, a big part, but the major momentum and activities to correct this issue must be led by the overall administrative leaders in order to impact all students.

Do you have misconceptions about suspension disproportionality?

Maybe. When we think about the over-suspension of some minority groups, a certain image comes to mind. The average person envisions a school with a highly diverse student population. As students are referred to the office for disciplinary incidents, we envision that different consequences—particularly suspensions—are meted out to students from different racial and ethnic groups.

This perception of suspension disproportionality may accurately reflect your district, but in many districts, it does not. In the U.S., unfortunately many schools are relatively monoracial or monoethnic while the district may be diverse. In some schools, the overwhelming majority of students may be from one racial or ethnic group. Some schools have a student body that is overwhelmingly white while other schools are predominantly African American or Hispanic etc.

I used to work in an enormously diverse school district. We had around 100,000 students, with the majority being African American. The English language learner population exceeded 10,000 students and was growing by 1,000 students a year. There were roughly 170 countries and 140 languages and dialects represented. We also had one of the largest refugee resettlement areas in the United States.

Even with such wonderful diversity on a district-wide basis, almost all of the schools were relatively monoracial or monoethnic. In fact, in all but a few schools, wide-ranging racial or ethnic diversity did not exist. The overwhelming majority of schools were almost exclusively African American. There were a few schools whose student body was almost exclusively white and a few schools had a majority of Hispanic students. So even in a school district that benefited from great diversity, that diversity did not exist at the local school. If similar enrollment patterns are found in your school district, you cannot see suspension disproportionality at the school level. It only becomes apparent when data are aggregated from across the entire district.

How does this impact our work?

Focus on clear communication and messaging. Many school principals ask, "How can my school be disproportionate? If I suspend virtually any student, they are going to be African American because my student body is almost exclusively African American." In such a school, the principal cannot see the disproportionality. There are virtually no students from different races and ethnicities with which to compare suspension patterns. The school administrator does not see a diverse group of students being referred to the office.

> **Do you have misperceptions about suspension disproportionality? Maybe.**

Therefore, you have to message that the suspension pattern in such a school far exceeds the suspension patterns found in other schools. Students (who in this example are African American) at this school have a greater risk of being suspended than students from other schools (who are not).

If this scenario is present in your school district, what should you do? Focus on those schools that have a high rate of suspension patterns, the schools that use suspensions at a much higher rate than other schools. Determine what actions steps can reduce suspensions in those schools and, more importantly, create a positive school culture.

Is PBIS the answer?

Maybe. Maybe not. Many conversations about suspension disproportionality lead to discussions about positive behavioral interventions and supports. I am confident that PBIS, when implemented with fidelity across a school, can increase students' appropriate behavior and reduce office discipline referrals and suspensions. Therefore, it is a very good thing.

The question is, though, does it impact racial and ethnic disproportionality? In order for PBIS to remedy suspension disproportionality, PBIS must reduce suspension rates more dramatically for some students than for others. If PBIS was equally implemented in all schools across a district with the same level of fidelity, does the variable of PBIS reduce suspension at a greater rate for the over-suspended group than for other students? If all groups of students see the same level of reduction in suspensions, the climate of the schools and overall student behavior may improve, but the statistical disproportionality remains the same.

I do not think we have clear and compelling evidence that PBIS has a greater impact on over-suspended student groups when compared to other groups. Over the last several years, thousands of schools have implemented PBIS. Many of these large cohorts have been sponsored, for lack of a better term, through federal grants or state departments of education. The data are certainly available to determine whether large-scale reductions in disproportionality have resulted from PBIS initiatives, but at the moment such clear evidence is unavailable. PBIS, when implemented with fidelity, is a very good thing. When equally applied to all schools, does PBIS correct disproportionality? Perhaps not.

There is another option. What if PBIS is not equally applied? What if schools in a district were ranked ranging from high to low suspension practices? Then, PBIS was applied only to those schools that had the highest suspension numbers. If those schools had a student body made up largely of students from the over-suspended group, then disproportionality could be reduced. It would never be appropriate to only apply PBIS to schools with higher populations of minority students.

In fact, making any decision about any student based on his race or ethnicity is wholly inappropriate. But if your district implements PBIS in schools with the highest suspension patterns, regardless of the racial or ethnic makeup of the student body, and a significant number of those schools are mostly made up of students from the over-suspended group, then disproportionality can theoretically be statistically and pragmatically impacted.

Is cultural competency the solution?

Many people propose cultural competency as the answer for correcting suspension disproportionality practices. To my knowledge, objective, replicable research is needed regarding this approach. That is not to say that it is unhelpful, but it certainly warrants further investigation before we determine its validity toward correcting suspension disproportionality.

Another barrier to this proposed solution might also exist. The common perception of disproportionality also contains the element of cross-racial suspensions and disciplinary actions. Some professionals assume that the teachers who refer students to the office and the school administrators who suspend the students are of a different race or ethnicity than the over-suspended students. This assumption may or may not be the case. If over-suspensions were caused by different races or ethnicities between the administrators or teachers and students, then we would expect to observe no suspension disproportionality in schools and in districts where teachers, administrators, and students share the same race or ethnic background.

Across the country, is suspension disproportionality evident in school districts in which the teachers, school administrators, and students are primarily the same race or ethnicity?

Unfortunately, yes. Suspension disproportionality exists in a wide variety of school districts where there is great diversity between the adults and students and also in districts where the adults and students are the same race and ethnicity. Therefore, the theory that cultural competence training would eliminate the over-suspension of some racial and ethnic groups might be suspect.

I certainly acknowledge that culture goes well beyond race and ethnicity. All members of the same racial or ethnic group do not share the same culture. Conversely, individuals who share the same culture can be of different races or of different ethnicities. I suggest that if you are considering cultural competency training as a corrective action for suspension disproportionality, determine if the vendor or the proponent of that approach can show that their work has reduced suspension disproportionality elsewhere.

Is suspension disproportionality caused by racism in our society, socioeconomic factors, high-risk neighborhoods, vulnerable family situations, or poor role models in our celebrity culture?

All of these factors and many other non-school issues probably contribute to suspension disproportionality. Many school personnel will want to spend a tremendous amount of time discussing non-school issues and how those factors must be corrected before we can truly move forward. Some of these points may be legitimate but we, as educators, cannot control them.

We would make much more progress in our schools if somehow all elements of our society were perfectly aligned to support our young people. In an ideal world, no racism would exist, and all of our students would leave stable homes every morning. There would be no poverty, and all famous athletes and actors would be good role models. That would be ideal, but it is not likely to happen. Even if our society makes no progress in these areas, we still have our obligations as educators. We must still find a way to improve our schools so that all of our students are supported and spend their time in class rather than in suspension. Lack of movement on our societal issues does not absolve us, as educators, of our obligation to reduce suspension disproportionality. A lack of progress does not absolve us from reducing suspension disproportionality.

The visual organizer has been updated to include all of the overarching instructional practices that I think set the foundation of specially designed instruction. The list provided thus far should be applied across subject and content areas. Again, feel free to develop your own list of practices for your school district. The point is that you should have a list that sets a strong foundation for your students and for your teachers. As an aside, you can ignore the "Don't Forget" box for now.

Great Instruction = Great Achievement

**Provide GREAT Instruction
(in every school,
in every class, every day)**

Guided by the performance standards

Rigorous with **R**esearch-based
practices

Engaging and exciting

Assessed continuously to guide
further instruction

Tailored in flexible groups

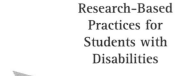

**Research-Based
Practices for
Students with
Disabilities**

- Effective universal
  instruction in all
  content areas
- Specially designed
  instruction

Don't Forget:

Specially Designed Instruction

All Classes	Mathematics	Co-Teaching
• Drastically increase practice turns and feedback • Provide explicit instruction • Provide explicit and embedded vocabulary instruction • Implement fill-the-gap interventions • Incorporate metacognitive instruction • Implement effective behavioral systems		

Guiding Questions

- In your school district, do teachers and administrators share a widespread understanding that expected behaviors must be taught routinely and that continual encouragement and feedback must be provided? If so, how do you see that common understanding operationalized? If not, what should happen in order for a shift to occur?

- In your school district, do leaders and teachers understand that behaviors are communicative and that they have a purpose? If so, how is that understanding operationalized? If not, why not?

- In your schools, what are the real goals for suspending a student? Are the suspensions effective at meeting your goals?

- Across your schools, do suspensions effectively change students' negative behaviors to more positive behaviors? (I am not referring to dangerous situations.) Support your answer with examples.

- In your school district, does suspension disproportionality exist for any racial or ethnic group of students with disabilities? If so, which racial or ethnic groups are affected?

- If the answer to the previous question is "yes," does suspension disproportionality exist for that same group when considering "all" students, not only students with disabilities? Cite the data used to answer this question.

- Using your school district's data management system, run a suspension report that includes each of your school's discipline patterns. A model of the report for fictional high schools is provided below. Include the same elements in your district-wide report. For this report, pull data from the last completed school year. Do not include student-specific information. For this purpose, only pull totals for each school. Include the total number of days assigned for ISS and OSS. This is different than the number of times that suspensions were assigned. This report references the number of days of instruction missed by the entire student body.

School	Total Student Population for the Last Completed School Year	Total Number of In-School-Suspension (ISS) days	Total Number of Out-of-School (OSS) days	Total Number of Suspension Days	Average Number of Suspension Days Assigned per Student in the Student Body
Parkridge High	1,250	650 Days	350 Days	1,000 Days	.80 Days
Mountainview High	1,350	980 Days	620 Days	1,600 Days	.84 Days
Redden High	1,110	540 Days	540 Days	1,080 Days	.97 Days
Douglas High	1,380	700 Days	450 Days	1,150 Days	.83 Days
Leyton High	1,200	840 Days	860 Days	1,700 Days	1.42 Days

After you run the report, sort data from highest to lowest suspension averages or total number of suspension days. Which schools have the highest rates of suspensions? How can you support those schools so that there is an improvement in student behavior and a reduction in suspensions?

- Using your data management system, for each school run a report that lists every student who was enrolled in your school for the most recently completed school year. For each student, include the total number of days that he or she was assigned in-school and out-of-school suspensions. For the sake of brevity, don't include those students who had zero suspension days. Also include totals and averages. A model is provided below. If the suspension patterns are troubling, what alternatives to suspensions can be used for misbehaviors that are bothersome but not dangerous?

Our School's Suspension Data

Student Name	Total Number of In-School Suspension Days Assigned	Total Number of Out-of-School Suspension Days Assigned	Total Number of Suspension Days Assigned
John Smith	12	7	19
Wanda Johnson	11	9	20
Tommy Leonard	13	10	23

VI
Math Instruction for Students with Disabilities

The last two chapters included recommendations regarding instructional practices that fortify the foundation of specially designed instruction, practices applicable to all classrooms. Let us now focus on the content area of mathematics because so many students with disabilities struggle in the area of math.

As far as math instruction is concerned, one question takes precedence over all others: "What instructional practices increase the achievement of our youngsters with disabilities in mathematics?" Fortunately, the National Mathematics Advisory Panel, referenced earlier in the book, answered that very question. As part of the panel's summary report, they succinctly described some powerful practices. Since I cannot summarize the panel's work any better than they can, I am including it verbatim.

Teaching Low-Achieving Students and Students with Learning Disabilities

The Panel conducted a review of 26 high-quality studies, mostly using randomized control designs. These studies provide a great deal of guidance concerning some defining features of effective instructional approaches for students with learning disabilities (LD) as well as low-achieving (LA) students. The review indicated that explicit methods of instruction are effective with LD and LA students.

Some key findings:
- *Explicit systematic instruction was found to improve the performance of students with learning disabilities in computation, solving word problems, and solving problems that require the application of mathematics to novel situations. Explicit systematic instruction typically entails teachers explaining and demonstrating specific strategies and allowing students many opportunities to ask and answer questions and to think aloud about the decisions they make while solving problems. It also entails careful sequencing of problems by the teacher or through instructional materials to highlight critical features. Significant positive effects were also found for Direct Instruction (a specific type of explicit instruction that provides teachers with scripts and that calls for frequent interactions between students and teachers, clear feedback to students on the accuracy of their work, and sequencing of problems so that critical differences are highlighted).*

- *Other forms of explicit systematic instruction have been developed with applications for students with learning disabilities. These developments reflect the infusion of research findings from cognitive psychology, with particular emphasis on automaticity and enhanced problem representation.*

- *Most of the small number of studies that investigated the use of visual representations yielded nonsignificant effects. However, studies that included visual representations along with the other components of explicit instruction tended to produce significant positive effects.*

Recommendation: The Panel recommends that students with learning disabilities and other students with learning problems receive, on a regular basis, some explicit systematic instruction that includes opportunities for students to ask and answer questions and think aloud about the decisions they make while solving problems. This kind of instruction should not comprise all the mathematics instruction these students receive. However, it does seem essential for building proficiency in both computation and the translation of word problems into appropriate mathematical equations and solutions. Some of this time should be dedicated to ensuring that students possess the foundational skills and conceptual knowledge necessary for understanding the mathematics they are learning at their grade level.

Recommendation: The Panel identified surprisingly few methodologically rigorous studies (given a literature base that spanned the past 30 years) that examined instructional practices designed to improve the performance of low-achieving students and students with learning disabilities. Although the actual quantity of such studies was small, their quality was high. There is a critical need for stimulating and supporting through federal funding of additional high-quality research to address this major national challenge. (2008)

Did anything jump out at you? Did you notice the panel makes recommendations for both students with learning disabilities in mathematics and for other students who struggle in math? Why is that? As I mentioned earlier (albeit sarcastically), anyone who has taught for longer than 16 seconds understands that sometimes students with disabilities and students without disabilities have similar instructional needs.

The panel also stated that explicit systematic instruction is beneficial. Sound familiar? Explicit instruction is one of our recommendations in all content areas for students with disabilities. It is encouraging to see that explicit systematic instruction is supported through rigorous research in the area of mathematics.

I appreciate how the panel described the components of explicit instruction. The terminology the panel uses is slightly different than the terminology used earlier (as referenced from Dr. Anita Archer), but the similarities are unmistakable. According to the panel, explicit systematic instruction includes the following elements:

- Demonstrating and modeling while the teacher "thinks aloud."
- Providing opportunities for students to ask questions and to receive answers and feedback.
- Careful sequencing of demonstrations and student work so that the most important elements are highlighted.
- Allowing students to think aloud as they complete math activities.

The panel clearly stated that all of the instruction the student receives should not be explicit and systematic. We do want youngsters to have some productive struggle with a little less structure provided by the teacher as they interact with mathematical concepts and applications. But math instruction for students with disabilities and other low-achieving math students must include explicit, systematic instruction routinely.

To what percentage of students do the panel's recommendations apply? We know that roughly 8-9% of students across the country are identified as having a disability and qualify for special education (U.S. Department of Education, 2014). The panel's recommendations apply to the portion of those students with disabilities who struggle in mathematics.

What percentage of other students are considered low-achieving math students? In the summary section of the report (p. xxiii), the panel concluded, "Explicit instruction with students who have mathematical difficulties has shown consistently positive effects on performance with word problems and computation. Results are consistent for students with learning disabilities, as well as other students who perform in the lowest third of a typical class."

Did you catch that—the lowest third of a typical class? We are not talking about a few isolated youngsters. If a middle school math class has 33 students, then roughly 11 of those students might not have disabilities but need systematic, explicit instruction. If you throw in a few students with disabilities, then a substantial percentage of youngsters need these instructional practices.

Unfortunately, in some school districts across the country, the pendulum of mathematics education appears to have oscillated very far indeed. I recently heard supposed math experts say, "It is not an instructional strategy unless students have come up with it on their own." Yikes! That may work for some students, but it certainly won't be effective for many students with disabilities or for other students who struggle in the area of mathematics.

Right now, in many places, we are in the middle of a purely constructivist approach to teaching mathematics. Many folks who are lauded as being knowledgeable in mathematics are defining effective math instruction as limited to a completely constructivist approach. They are openly stating that explicit, systematic instruction is a bad thing.

With this message, I'm afraid we are going to see many students continue to struggle in math. I look forward to the day when the math instruction pendulum returns to a place where a more balanced approach is accepted. The visual organizer has now been updated to include the specific foundational elements of specially designed instruction that should be in place in math classes to increase the achievement of our students with disabilities.

Great Instruction = Great Achievement

Provide GREAT Instruction (in every school, in every class, every day)

Guided by the performance standards

Rigorous with Research-based practices

Engaging and exciting

Assessed continuously to guide further instruction

Tailored in flexible groups

Research-Based Practices for Students with Disabilities

- Effective universal instruction in all content areas
- Specially designed instruction

Don't Forget:

Specially Designed Instruction

All Classes	Mathematics	Co-Teaching
• Drastically increase practice turns and feedback • Provide explicit instruction • Provide explicit and embedded vocabulary instruction • Implement fill-the-gap interventions • Incorporate metacognitive instruction • Implement effective behavioral systems	• Provide systematic and explicit instruction • Model with teacher think-aloud and promote and expect students to think aloud	

Guiding Questions

- In your school district's math classes, are students with disabilities and other students who struggle provided systematic, explicit instruction that includes:

  - Providing opportunities for students to ask questions and to receive answers and feedback.

  - Careful sequencing of demonstrations and student work so that the most important elements are highlighted.

  - Allowing students to think aloud as they complete math activities.

  Justify your answer.

- Has ongoing training, support, and coaching been provided to general education and special education teachers regarding systematic and explicit instruction?

VII
Effective Co-Teaching

Over the last 15 years or so, there has been a significant increase in the percentage of students with disabilities who receive their instruction in general education classes. In many of those classes, co-teaching is occurring. A general education and special education teacher share responsibilities for educating every student in the class, those with and without disabilities.

Was your school district like many others? Did you see an initial increase in the achievement of your students with disabilities when your district increased efforts toward inclusion? Most districts did. An immediate bump in performance occurred when students with disabilities received instruction in regular education classrooms beside their non-disabled peers.

I have seen evidence of this bump in district after district, and I have some theories that might explain it. First, students began to receive instruction from teachers who were deeply knowledgeable of the content area and of the specific standards for that grade. Second, there is a natural set of higher expectations in most general education classes when compared to some pull-out classes in the same schools.

It isn't intentional. Special education teachers do not purposely lower their expectations for youngsters with disabilities, but a softening of expectations occurs gradually over time. When the bulk of the students you teach have disabilities and struggle with learning, it is very easy to forget how advanced many typically developing students are. In some pull-out special education classes, a hum of low expectations pervades the atmosphere.

The low expectations can also be attributed to the students themselves. When many students with disabilities enter general education classes, they immediately have higher self-expectations because they begin to work with their non-disabled peers. They think to themselves, "If all these guys can do it, then I can do it too."

So when more students with disabilities were initially educated in general education classrooms, which were often co-teaching classrooms, our students with disabilities experienced a natural increase in achievement. Unfortunately, in many districts that increase in achievement plateaued after a few years. Why the plateau? In many places, the co-teaching practices reached a certain level of effectiveness but then leveled out.

Increasing our students' access to general education classes is a wonderful accomplishment. As a nation, we have made much progress over the last 15 years or so, but we need to keep pushing the performance envelope. The upward trend in achievement will not continue if we fail to consistently enhance the co-teaching practices and techniques. (We must also realize that some students with disabilities will continue to need some pull-out special education instruction.)

The first year I co-taught was in 1991. I taught students with orthopedic impairments in a wonderful, little elementary school. I co-taught in the areas of science and social studies with a very talented general education teacher. When I began teaching at the middle-school level, I co-taught all of the elective, or connection, classes. Admittedly, I had very little content knowledge in home economics (now known as consumer sciences), or in any of those elective classes, but my co-teachers and I did fairly well based on what we knew about effective co-teaching at that time. Fortunately, my understanding of how to effectively co-teach has improved substantially since then.

Before we dig into co-teaching, close your eyes and think about the last co-teaching class that you observed. As special education administrators, you are probably in classrooms fairly frequently if only for a few minutes at a time. What did you see? What were the *teachers* doing?

You might have observed one of the teachers taking the instructional lead while the other teacher circulated around the room to help individual students. Perhaps you observed a "better" co-teaching scenario in which both teachers were bouncing off of each other, finishing each other's sentences, and providing different perspectives as they shared the teaching for a whole group of students. Most of us would probably agree that the second co-teaching classroom is much better than the first. After all, I have often heard that there is good co-teaching technique when you "can't tell the special education teacher from the general education teacher."

I agree that the first scenario is not very advanced. If one teacher is primarily circulating around the room and helping individual students, then you are not really getting much bang for the buck. The students are not really receiving a tremendous amount of added benefit from having two teachers in the room. So, the second scenario is *much* better, right?

Not so fast. The second scenario might be a *little* better, but not by much. Neither of these scenarios is sufficient. For a number of years now, we have held the second scenario up as one of the ultimate forms of co-teaching, but should we? Now, close your eyes and return to that observation where the teachers were sharing teaching responsibilities, interchanging ideas, and working smoothly together with the entire class. What were the *students* doing in the second scenario?

Even though the teachers are working fluidly at the front of the room and sharing the teaching responsibilities, the *students* are really doing the same thing that they would be doing with only a single teacher in the room. Each student is still part of a large group, and each student participates in whole group activities. Wait a minute. In those classes where it is clear the co-teachers have spent time co-planning and are both engaged and sharing the teaching from the front of the room, the students are not actually doing anything differently than they would if there was only a single teacher in the room. So what are the benefits of having two teachers in the classroom? In reality, there aren't many.

Remember, teaching is not about what the teacher does. It is about what the students do. (In fact, doesn't that apply to all instructional practices?) Students learn through having GREAT instruction. Part of that instruction is the quality and quantity of the practice turns and feedback that they experience. In the shared teaching scenario, the teachers have worked tirelessly and it may be seamless to watch, but all of that effort might be in vain if the students' learning activities do not change.

What is the benefit of having two teachers in the classroom if the students' learning activities are not drastically improved? Especially when you think of this purely from a pragmatic, budget-driven perspective: Why are you paying two teachers to do the job that one teacher can do?

When you have two teachers in the classroom, you should see small-group instruction routinely. Each of the teachers should be leading a small group of students in an instructional activity at the same time. There can also be independent student groups. Sound familiar? I mentioned this in the section about practice turns and feedback.

If you have a class of 30 students and only 1 teacher, the student-teacher ratio is 30 to 1. If you have two co-teachers who teach from the front of the room, no matter how masterfully, the *active* student-teacher ratio continues to be 30 to 1.

If each of those teachers routinely leads small-group instruction, the ratio becomes 15 to 1. If there are rotating student independent groups, the ratio is generally reduced to 10 to 1. (These numbers will be different if the different groups have different numbers of students, and they should.)

What a difference small-group instruction makes! With the addition of another teacher, the instruction and student activities should naturally change. With 10 students in your group, you can plan differentiated activities that are crafted to meet the needs of the students in each group. Each student can increase their practice turns and get a higher quality and quantity of effective feedback. Now we're talking!

The instructional groups should be flexible and tailored. (Remember the "T" in GREAT instruction?) The special education teacher should not teach only the students with disabilities and the general education teacher should not only teach the students who do not have IEPs.

Both teachers are equally and fully responsible for the education of all students in their class. Both groups are flexible and determined by the students' ongoing needs. All groups include students with and without disabilities. Sometimes, the groups will be homogenous, where students have similar instructional levels on a given topic, and sometimes, the groups will be heterogeneous, where students function with different skillfulness.

The different teachers will bring different expertise to the classroom, of course. Often, the special education teacher has more expertise in altering pedagogy to meet the needs of a variety of youngsters whereas the general education teacher typically has more expertise in the content area. These statements are generalities and certainly not always true.

During their co-teaching, both teachers should gain experience and expertise. The special education teacher should gain knowledge in the content area while the general education teacher should expand her expertise in pedagogy. I do not agree with the opinion that special education teachers do not need to learn the content because they are the instructional support professionals. If we expect high school students to learn biology, for example, then we can expect a special education teacher, who has at least a bachelor's degree, to gain knowledge in this content area over time. Likewise, we can expect the general education teacher to broaden her pedagogical repertoire. Both teachers should be expected to broaden their skills.

This approach requires common planning time. When the school schedule is originally developed months before the school year even starts, students with disabilities should be placed first on the master schedule in their co-teaching and pull-out special education classes. At that time, common planning time for each co-teaching team should be placed on the schedule. If you don't prioritize the master schedule in this way, it will be nearly impossible to insert common planning periods at a later date.

There is another reason for expecting small-group instruction in co-teaching classes. When a student's IEP indicates that he will participate in a co-teaching class, we are making an obligation to the parent. We are stating that the student will receive specially designed instruction in that co-teaching classroom. Yes, specially designed instruction should be occurring in the general education, co-teaching classroom. In the second scenario above, when both teachers are leading the instruction with the whole group, what is so specialized about that? Absolutely nothing.

Here is where we make the connection. What specially designed instruction should those special education teachers (and really the general education teachers also) be providing in those co-teaching classes? Remember that list we spent a significant amount of this book describing? In that co-teaching class, the teachers should drastically increase practice turns and feedback, provide effective vocabulary instruction, implement positive behavioral systems, provide metacognitive instruction, and so on. See how it all connects?

By creating a list of instructional practices that form the foundation of specially designed instruction and by requiring co-teachers to routinely lead small-group instruction, and including those specially designed instructional practices in those small groups, then we will certainly help increase student learning.

Which students should receive that instruction? Perhaps all of them to different degrees. Most students with disabilities need those instructional practices, but so do many students who struggle but do not qualify for such services. In addition, the instructional practices can be tailored to meet the needs of high-performing students as well.

Let me add a couple additional suggestions from hard-earned experiences. Before you start implementing this message and related training regarding co-teaching classes, conduct observations in a wide-ranging

> **When you have two teachers in the classroom, you should see small-group instruction routinely. Each of the teachers should be leading a small-group of students in an instructional activity. There can also be independent student groups.**

selection of classes across your district. When people do this, they are often surprised to discover only one teacher in a co-teaching classroom. The special education teacher might be substituting for a sick colleague, or the general education teacher might be "running his errands" around the school during class time.

If you happen to find co-teachers going it alone, then work with principals to set a new standard. Both co-teachers must be in the co-teaching classroom for the entire class period. This is not optional. Even though I think we can sometimes overplay the compliance card, this is a good time to use it. If co-teaching is in a student's IEP and the student is not participating in a class with both teachers, then there is, indeed, a very real problem. The student is not receiving the services outlined in her IEP. A student with a disability is not getting the services she needs.

Now, another piece of advice. When you roll out the training and support regarding co-teaching, take some of the models off of the table (Brown, 2004). It doesn't matter whether you are using the six models of co-teaching as described by Friend and Burrello (2005) or the four models outlined by Villa and Thousands (2013), you must limit the options for the co-teaching pairs.

If you train personnel on all of the models, including the models where one teacher moves around the room or when both teachers share teaching from the front of the room, you will find it very difficult to improve beyond those two scenarios.

You should make it clear from the very start that effective co-teaching includes small-group instruction in those classes. Start there and build all training, coaching, follow-up, and monitoring around that theme, and you will have a much greater chance of seeing best practices adopted across your district's co-teaching classes. Small-group instruction, with each teacher routinely leading groups at the same time, is established as an expectation from the start and should occur routinely.

You will get pushback, of course. Some of the pushback will come from special education teachers and some will come from their general education colleagues. Change is often difficult. There are issues of mutual trust, perceived competencies, loss of control, and adoption of new roles, among others.

At the beginning of the co-teaching partnership, there should be an investment of time in which the teachers can get together and have critical conversations. What are their fundamental beliefs about students, instruction, and pedagogy? How do they prefer to run a classroom: taking attendance, setting classroom expectations, turning in homework, responding to students' needs, allowing students to go to the bathroom, etc.? Through these conversations, a partnership can develop, which is a critical element of any co-teaching environment.

Make no mistake, however. Co-teaching is not about implementing what is easiest or best for the adults. It is implemented when students *need* something that any single teacher cannot provide. Therefore, as special education administrators, we have to start with that frame of reference, and share it with our principals and our co-teachers. This is the pitch I usually use:

"There are students in your schools that can absolutely master grade-level work. They can do it! But they *need* both teachers. One teacher working in isolation, or two teachers taking turns, or two teachers delivering the same instruction that can be provided by one teacher, will not be sufficient. They need *both* of you.

"In your classes, there are tall students, short students, gifted athletes, good readers, insightful minds, talented musicians, and great storytellers. Every single student in your class has gifts and talents that will contribute to other students' experiences and to the class as a whole. In addition, every student in your class has weaknesses, and some have disabilities. It is part of the human condition. They all need both of you—the general education teacher and the special education teacher. Both of you must bring your respective talents, experience, expertise, and perspective. They will need all of that to become who they need to become. Every student in your class has two teachers. Every student in this class belongs to both of you. There are no visitors here. Every student belongs, and both teachers are needed.

"During this co-teaching journey, we want your classroom to reflect something that neither of you could accomplish alone. As a matter of routine, we should see small-group instruction. Both of you should lead small groups at the same time. In those groups, your students should try new skills, refine those skills, and become masters in our standards. We also expect to see student independent groups.

"In your class, none of those groups will be stagnant and they won't consist of 'Ms. Smith's students' and 'Ms. Johnson's students.' The groups will be flexible, and students will move from different groups as their needs dictate. In those groups, we want students doing, not receiving. They should actively be engaged in actions; they should be receiving brainstorming and feedback from one another, you, technology, and from themselves as they become more and more accomplished in their work.

"In order for that to happen, you will have to develop a deep partnership. You will plan together, brainstorm together, refine together, hopefully laugh together, face barriers together, and celebrate together. You will probably get frustrated with each other. When that happens, simmer down and take as much time as you need to decompress, and then when you are ready, talk to your partner about it. Don't let it percolate and build up. Like every relationship that is worth having, it will take work.

"But remember, the students need this. They cannot make it to where they are supposed to go, to who they are supposed to become, without both of you. Neither one of you can meet all of their needs. They need all of both of you.

"It is important that you know I believe you can do this. I know that you can be successful. I have great confidence that you can help each other. All of your students will not only grow but thrive! You can do this, and I can't wait to watch this journey unfold."

As special education administrators, you can set this foundation and provide the needed support to your principals, assistant principals, and co-teachers as they make great things happen with children. You can lead this. The visual organizer has been updated to include big messages about effective co-teaching.

Great Instruction = Great Achievement

Provide GREAT Instruction (in every school, in every class, every day)

Guided by the performance standards

Rigorous with Research-based practices

Engaging and exciting

Assessed continuously to guide further instruction

Tailored in flexible groups

Research-Based Practices for Students with Disabilities

- Effective universal instruction in all content areas
- Specially designed instruction

Don't Forget:

Specially Designed Instruction

All Classes	Mathematics	Co-Teaching
• Drastically increase practice turns and feedback • Provide explicit instruction • Provide explicit and embedded vocabulary instruction • Implement fill-the-gap interventions • Incorporate metacognitive instruction • Implement effective behavioral systems	• Provide systematic and explicit instruction • Model with teacher think-aloud and promote and expect students to think aloud • Reinforce effort rather than misperceived innate ability	• Both teachers should lead small-group instruction at the same time • There can also be student independent groups • Specially designed instructional practices should be implemented in the small groups

Guiding Questions

- In your school district, did you see an increase in achievement when you significantly increased the percentage of students who were educated in general education classes? If so, why do you think the increase occurred?

- Did you experience a plateau in the achievement of students with disabilities a couple years after you transitioned more students into general education classes? If so, what do you think caused the plateau?

- In your schools, what do you see in a typical co-teaching class? What are the teachers doing? What are the students doing?

- In your role as special education leaders, have you provided a clear message that co-teaching should involve both teachers routinely leading small-group instruction at the same time? Is that a central message regarding all co-teaching training, follow-up, support, coaching, etc.? If not, how can you build and deliver that core message?

- Is there a clear understanding that students with disabilities who are educated in co-teaching classes, per their IEP, should receive specially designed instruction in those classes? What does that look like in most of your co-teaching classes?

- When training has occurred for co-teaching teams, what messages have been communicated to co-teachers regarding specific instructional practices that they should implement in their classes (beyond the co-teaching models)? Does your district promote a list of specific instructional practices that meet the requirement of specially designed instruction while simultaneously meeting the needs of students without disabilities? If not, how can you move forward toward that goal?

VIII
Student Attendance

You might have noticed that our visual organizer has some missing information. Let's address student attendance. Technically, it does not fall under the different elements of GREAT instruction or research-based instructional practices, yet absences have a tremendous negative impact on so many youngsters—those with and without disabilities.

Personnel from the Georgia Department of Education (Woods, 2016) analyzed data regarding student attendance and graduation rates. They reviewed the data for all students (not just students with disabilities) across Georgia who should have graduated from high school after four years. Then they went back to those students' ninth-grade year to review their attendance patterns. This study included thousands of students across the state. They included every student who was enrolled continuously in Georgia high schools, even if the students transferred among many different schools or across several districts.

What are your guesses? What percentage of students who had zero absences during their ninth-grade year do you suppose earned a diploma four years later? What about those students who had 1-5 absences or 11-15 absences? What was the graduation rate among those students who were absent for 15 or more days their freshman year? The following information is revealing.

Table 2.1 Student Absences in Ninth Grade and Graduation Rates in Four Years

Number of Absences During Ninth Grade	Percentage of Students Who Graduated in Four Years
0	80.52%
1-5	82.24%
6-10	72.68%
11-14	61.27%
15 or more	30.73%

It is important to note that the study included all absences—excused and unexcused absences. It also included out-of-school suspensions. Of those students who had zero absences in ninth grade, roughly 81% graduated with a high school diploma four years later. To be honest, that surprised me. With a perfect attendance record in ninth grade, I assumed that the graduation rate would be close to 100%, but I was wrong.

Many years ago, high schools were much less rigorous. Most high schools had a low-level track that would still enable a student to earn a high school diploma and matriculate to college. Some students took algebra over multiple semesters or years, for example, and earned another math course by taking a low-level home budgeting class.

That is no longer the case. For many years now, our students have experienced a steady increase in academic rigor. Not only do students need to attend class on a consistent basis, they need to work diligently to master high school standards. (Admittedly, high school is still not rigorous enough for some students.) In addition, our schools must provide effective instruction routinely. Taking all these factors into account, students need to attend school regularly, work diligently, and participate in effective instruction in order to make sufficient progress. Attendance alone is insufficient.

When students had between 1-5 absences their freshman year, the graduation rate increased slightly, but the difference was not statistically significant (McGiboney, 2016). Even though the study did not include an analysis of the reasons for the absences, perhaps we can apply some common sense. When a student attends school every day during the school year or misses 1-5 days during the school year, it does not reflect a pattern. Students get sick a few days each year. They get their braces put on and have the occasional injury. They are not consistently missing instruction. In essence, 1-5 absences in a school year does not diminish access to the curriculum or instruction.

With 6 to 10 absences, we begin to see a pattern and the corresponding effect. We see a slide in the graduation rate. What happens for a student who struggles in math and misses three days of instruction during that algebra class? What happens if those absences are during the third week of school? The student misses extremely important instruction and has a hard time connecting the dots. A deep hole is created. How impactful is it if a student missed two days in a row in a high school that has block scheduling? In some schools, that is actually missing four days of the material.

After each additional absence following the fifth absence, the loss of achievement grows considerably. For the group of students who had 15 or more days of absences during their freshman year, only 31% earned a diploma four years later. Again, the data included both excused and unexcused absences along with out-of-school suspensions. Therefore, even when students miss school for acceptable reasons, they still miss valuable instruction.

When you think of students who had 15 or more absences, do you see a face? Regardless of whether you work in an elementary school, middle school, high school, or at the central office, do you know youngsters who are going to be absent for 15 or more days this year? Unfortunately, you probably see many faces.

This study and others like it show us that students who miss school have lower graduation rates. Perhaps such a finding is not all that newsworthy. What is newsworthy, however, is how the study reveals a lower graduation rate among students with as few as 6 absences as opposed to students with fewer absences. Six absences is a relatively low number, perhaps fewer than many of us would suspect to be reflected in graduation rates. It should be noted, of course, that the study cannot establish direct causality between absenteeism and graduation rates. Perhaps there is a correlation. Students who miss school regularly might have an array of risk factors that contribute to their underachievement.

The Georgia Department of Education study also looked at eighth-grade absences. Not surprisingly, the relationship between graduation rates and the eighth-grade attendance data were very similar.

Table 2.2 Student Absences in Eighth Grade and Graduation Rates in Four Years

Number of Absences During Eighth Grade	Percentage of Students Who Graduated in Four Years
0	81.89%
1-5	80.17%
6-10	71.91%
11-14	61.08%
15 or more	38.09%

What Should We Do About Student Absences?

The truth is that we have little research regarding how to improve student attendance. Several entities have published guiding principles which may be helpful, but we do not have many known practices that have consistently been found, through rigorous and repeated research, to improve student attendance. Therefore, we need to use common sense and adopt a practical approach.

Analyze Data

First, you have to review your school's and district's attendance data. Let me provide a warning here. When schools review their attendance data, they often look at the ADAR (Average Daily Attendance Rate). This rate represents the average percentage of enrolled students who are present each day over a certain time period.

Very often, you will meet school personnel who state, "We don't have an attendance problem. Our ADAR is 95%." That sounds good, right? Throughout all my years of working in education, 95% has always been a good grade. That is a good, solid "A."

Not so fast. Those results are not as promising as they might appear. If a school has a 95% ADAR, during the average school day, 95% of the students are in attendance. That translates to 1 absence for every 20 students on a daily basis. To shape it in a different way, on average, each student misses one out of every 20 school days (Keltz, 2013). Perhaps the celebration is a little premature.

If every student, on average, misses one out of every 20 school days, then students are missing nine days out of a typical 180-day school year. With nine absences, they are in the group of students with a rounded 73% graduation rate (if we apply the Georgia Department of Education research findings regarding ninth-grade absences). That misleading ADAR, which at first looked positive, is actually quite troubling. Because it is so counterintuitive to think of 95% as a troubling score, for many professionals it is best to scuttle ADAR all together.

It is much more productive to examine attendance data using the same categories defined by the Georgia Department of Education study. Look at the theoretical high school below with a total student population of 2,000 students with 500 freshmen. The attendance data for the ninth graders are provided.

Table 2.3 Achievement High School Attendance Data – Percentage of Ninth-Grade Students Who Missed Days of School Last School Year

0 Absences		1-5 Absences		6-10 Absences		11-14 Absences		15 or More Absences	
# of Students	% of Students	# of Students	% of Students	# of Students	% of Students	# of Students	% of Students	# of Students	% of Students
60	12%	200	40%	150	30%	65	13%	25	5%

At Achievement High, there was a 95% ADAR for the ninth graders' last school year. When we examine the data more closely, it becomes clear how the seemingly impressive ADAR provides a false sense of security. 30% of the freshman, or 150 students, accumulated 6-10 absences. Another 65 students had 11-14 absences, and 25 members of the freshman class missed 15 or more days of school. If we use the Georgia Department of Education study to forecast graduation rates for this freshman class, these are the rates we can expect:

- Only 109 of the 150 students who accumulated 6-10 absences will earn a diploma in four years.
- 40 of the 65 students with 11-14 absences will graduate on time.
- 10 of the 25 students who missed 15 or more days will walk during graduation ceremonies.

This paints a drastically different picture than the vaunted 95% ADAR. Instead of celebrating the attendance patterns at Achievement High, there is real cause for concern. The school must partner with students and families to implement activities that improve student attendance. It does not matter whether or not GREAT instruction is occurring when students do not come to school. Students need to participate in GREAT instruction in order to benefit from it.

Tiered Initiatives and Interventions to Address Attendance

It is helpful to look at attendance through the same lens that we view Response to Intervention (RTI) or a Multi-Tiered System of Supports (MTSS).

In my experience, across most schools, more than 30% of students miss more than five days of school which has a correlation to decreased odds of earning a high school diploma. Therefore, schools should implement Tier 1 or universal initiatives to promote school attendance. There can be social messaging campaigns, partnerships with the PTA or PTO, signed agreements with parents and students, class and grade competitions, and training for all stakeholders regarding the negative impact of missing school. There can also be partnerships with the community.

At different student ages, the initiatives will vary. At the elementary level, school attendance is primarily a parent issue. Second graders do not wake themselves or drive themselves to school. In order to increase student attendance and to reduce absences, schools must have a wide-reaching and positive messaging system and partnership with parents to set a universal or Tier 1 foundation.

> For the group of students who had 15 or more days of absences during their freshman year, only 31% earned a high school diploma in four years.
>
> Georgia Department of Education

In high school and, to a lesser degree, in middle school, student absences can be a student issue in addition to a parent issue. Unfortunately, some high school students skip school or create self-imposed barriers for their own attendance. In high school, the school-wide campaign must speak directly to students, but parents should not be left out of the campaign. In fact, parent involvement is critical, but student partnership is also important.

Just as you would in any MTSS or RTI model, you must provide more intensive interventions for students and families who are not progressing sufficiently as a result of the school-wide attendance efforts. You should implement specific interventions like meeting with parents and students individually, developing contracts, and so on. By using a tiered approach, student attendance can improve.

A component of implementing any intervention is determining why the student is having difficulty. If Jonah has a very ill parent and is spending lots of time at the hospital, the actions of the school will take a certain path. On the other hand, if Trey is missing school because he plays video games through the night, the interventions and actions will be different. Interventions should always respond to the needs of the student and his family.

When should attendance interventions begin for specific students? Before the school year even starts! We have at least one full year of attendance data for many of our students. In most schools, a large percentage of the student body attended the same school the prior year. Many other students attended other schools in the same district, albeit at a different school. The attendance records for all of these students can be found using the district's data management system.

By examining attendance data from the previous school year, we can identify those students with a pattern of low attendance. We do not have to wait until that pattern emerges once again in the new school year. We can start interventions for those specific students before the school year starts.

How powerful would it be if the school invited those students and families who have a high absentee rate to a meeting before the first day of school? The tone of the meeting would need to be very positive, of course. School personnel can stress how Johnny is such an important member of the school family. Without Johnny, the school community is incomplete. In fact, Johnny is needed for very important jobs in the school. He can be a member of the school's news team that broadcasts announcements every morning (Jolie Hardin, 2014). In order to do that, he needs to arrive every school day on time in order to provide this very important service to his fellow schoolmates. This type of positive engagement and attachment can shape the habits of the student and parents regarding school attendance.

Out-of-School Suspensions

In addition to the school-wide initiatives and targeted attendance interventions for some students, we must have the courage to look at our own professional practices. We must analyze our use of out-of-school suspensions (OSSs). In some schools, suspending students for misbehavior is commonplace. It has become the only tool in the disciplinary toolbox.

An earlier chapter included information regarding in-school and out-of-school suspensions. Please refer to that chapter to learn more about the alternatives to suspension that can have a more effective impact than suspending students. Even though school suspension is sometimes appropriate, please be aware of the double jeopardy that is happening for the student. Not only is Charlie receiving suspension days, he is also missing valuable instruction. The research on the impact of missing school makes clear that by suspending Charlie, we are decreasing the likelihood of his success when he returns.

I am not asking schools to completely end all suspensions. I do want suspensions to be only one of many tools in the disciplinary toolbox. I also want schools to be extremely purposeful with their consequences, and to understand how a few missed days of instruction can potentially correlate to a student's reduced chances of earning a high school diploma. It is difficult for any child to regroup academically if he is suspended for three, five, or eight days and misses the corresponding instruction.

We want to provide consequences for students when it is warranted. We have the responsibility to help youngsters understand that behaviors—both good and bad behaviors—have consequences. We want to make sure those consequences actually have a high probability that the negative behavior will be reduced and also that we don't create enormous barriers for students, through missed instruction, so that they cannot be successful. That will only increase negative behaviors.

The visual organizer has been updated. In order to increase the achievement of students with disabilities, we must promote increases in attendance. The recommendations described above have been added below.

Great Instruction = Great Achievement

Provide GREAT Instruction
(in every school,
in every class, every day)

Guided by the performance standards

Rigorous with Research-based practices

Engaging and exciting

Assessed continuously to guide further instruction

Tailored in flexible groups

Research-Based Practices for Students with Disabilities

- Effective universal instruction in all content areas
- Specially designed instruction

Don't Forget:

- Implement school-wide attendance initiatives
- Provide tiered actions for specific students
- Utilize alternatives to suspensions to shape students' behaviors

Specially Designed Instruction

All Classes	Mathematics	Co-Teaching
• Drastically increase practice turns and feedback • Provide explicit instruction • Provide explicit and embedded vocabulary instruction • Implement fill-the-gap interventions • Incorporate metacognitive instruction • Implement effective behavioral systems	• Provide systematic and explicit instruction • Model with teacher think-aloud and promote and expect students to think aloud • Reinforce effort rather than misperceived innate ability	• Both teachers should lead small-group instruction at the same time • There can also be student independent groups • Specially designed instructional practices should be implemented in the small groups

Guiding Questions

- Complete the chart below for the most recently completed school year.

Our School's or District's Attendance Data

Number of Absences for the Most Recently Completed School Year	Number of Students	Percentage of Overall Student Population
0		
1-5		
6-10		
11-14		
15 or more		

- What are your reactions to the data above?

- The data from the study described in this chapter showed the impact that absences can have on graduation rates. The study included all students. How do you think absences impact the learning or graduation rates for students with disabilities in comparison to students without disabilities?

- As a central office leader, how can you share your district's data with other leaders in order to have an impact on attendance patterns?

Section 2:
10 Steps to Making It Happen

For the first half of this book, we have responded to the superintendent's inquiry, "We have to radically increase the achievement of students with disabilities. What should we do?" We must implement GREAT instruction in every school, in every class, for every child, every day. For students with disabilities, that means we have to implement research-based practices in two ways. We have to provide an extremely strong core instructional program. Then we have to build a foundation of specially designed instruction by focusing on a specific list of instructional practices that have a significant impact on the achievement of students with disabilities. Those instructional practices should be seen routinely in general education classes with one teacher, co-teaching classes, and pull-out classes.

But that is only half of the work. Knowing what to do is extremely important, but only gets us so far. As special education administrators, how do we make it happen? How, as special education leaders, do we become agents of change? How do we go from ideas to action and outcomes?

During the remainder of this book, you will read about the 10 steps needed in order to implement this work. These 10 steps are critical and specifically designed for special education administrators. There is a caution. Even though the steps are presented in sequential form, they are not linear. You will be spinning several plates simultaneously.

Also, the ultimate plan is to develop a wave of momentum that is actually led by the curriculum and instruction department and other offices (i.e., the supervisors of principals) with tremendous support from your team. The work described in the next chapters is the groundwork that your team must complete so that the overall momentum is created and persists. These steps prepare the special education department to create a context and environment where impacting the achievement of students with disabilities, and other students who struggle, is a priority for all educators across your district.

IX
Step 1: Alter Your Focus

You might suspect that we jump right into training staff. Not so fast. If we are going to make long-term change across the district, we have to help transform the way the central office, school leaders, and teachers approach their work. Several of the steps will focus on things that you do before you provide any formal training.

Step 1: Alter Your Focus

First, you must alter your focus. Over the last four decades in special education, the federal IDEA legislation has become more and more complex with every revision. The regulations have become incredibly expansive and in many states, the state departments of education have added additional required activities. We are drowning in compliance.

In addition, there are extensive responsibilities that fall under the category of daily operations. We must develop budgets, ensure that our special education programs are fully staffed, analyze and order specialized instructional materials, work with the transportation department to ensure that students' needs are met, etc. etc. etc.

What has resulted? In my opinion, the overwhelming majority of special education departments across the country have become almost entirely focused on compliance and daily operations activities. You will certainly hear special education administrators say, "I wish I could devote some time to improving instruction, but I can't get to it." There is absolutely a great deal of truth to that. Compliance and daily operations activities are virtually impossible to complete because of the sheer breadth of those demands. Our focus, not because of our own choice, has been devoted exhaustingly to these activities.

Unfortunately, as we consider the big three buckets of our work—compliance activities, daily operations, and instruction—our work hours could be represented by the following graphic:

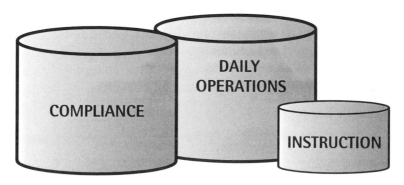

As special education leaders, we have to take control of this. We can certainly lobby for less complicated federal legislation and state requirements, and we should, but we also have to re-focus our own work. If we plan to become instructional leaders *after* all of the compliance and daily operation activities are completed, frankly, we will *never* become instructional leaders.

The most impactful thing that we can do for students with disabilities is to provide GREAT instruction. Powerful, research-based instruction is a life changer for students. Yet, in many special education departments, that is not our focus. The expansiveness of the regulatory requirements and the demands of daily operations certainly earn some blame for this, but we, as special education administrators, also have to own our part.

Some current special education administrators actually feel much more comfortable implementing daily operations and compliance activities than leading instructional change. In many districts, after years as a leader in special education, many administrators feel much less comfortable brainstorming a child's challenges with grasping science concepts than leading a series of tense IEP meetings.

> **If we plan to become instructional leaders after all of the compliance and daily operations activities are completed, frankly, we will never become instructional leaders.**

This might apply to you. Perhaps you have gained many administrative skills, but your instructional expertise has become rusty. I'm not saying that most special education administrators weren't strong teachers. Most were. In fact, most special education directors I have met were *naturally* strong teachers.

You have met these teachers. They enter their first classroom and they just understand the work. They are adept at maintaining classroom management, inspiring students, and systematically providing instruction that increases student learning. It is amazing to watch someone who is a *natural*.

Unfortunately, most of our special education and general education teachers do not arrive at proficiency naturally. They have to learn their craft. They need personnel in their schools and in their districts who can systematically help them become stronger teachers.

Sometimes, those *natural* teachers are not the best instructional leaders. Being natural at something does not mean that you know how to help others. In fact, sometimes individuals who come to a task through some natural talent do not know the science and research behind what they do. They naturally impact youngsters and provide effective instruction, but they don't know why what they do is effective.

Several years ago, I had a friend who had a bachelor's degree in engineering from a highly respected school of engineering and an MBA in business. He was naturally (and through hard work) extremely strong at mathematics. During his mid-30s, he felt called to be a teacher. Once he earned his certification and started teaching high school math, he had a difficult time. He could not understand how students could struggle with mathematics. It was so effortless for him that he didn't know how to break it down for struggling learners. To oversimplify, he often didn't know how he arrived at an answer or how he jumped a few steps forward in the problem solving process. He just did it.

Just like my friend, a naturally talented teacher may not know how she has an impact on her students or why what she does is so effective. Just because a special education administrator was a strong, and perhaps naturally gifted, teacher does not mean that she is an effective *instructional leader.*

In addition, in some school districts we have promoted coordinators and special education lead teachers for the wrong reasons. Recently, I posted a vacancy for a somewhat lead teacher of special education position. I received several references about a particular teacher from a neighboring school district's special education department where I have several colleagues. They made a point to contact me about this applicant. They gave extremely strong references for this potential employee. They expounded on how this candidate would be the perfect fit for the job. She apparently had great ability in completing compliance activities. In addition, this teacher had performed beautifully in ongoing, escalated IEP meetings.

When I asked each reference (who were all part of that district's special education department) about the applicant's skills and knowledge in instruction, each of them told me that they could not comment on those skills because they weren't familiar with her teaching practices.

In essence, several members of the central office special education department in this neighboring school district strongly recommended this candidate who had excellent skills related to implementing compliance activities, but had no knowledge regarding her instructional capacity. Their perspective was obvious. A strong special education leader is someone who is outstanding at compliance and daily operations. Instructional skillfulness is not even considered.

I am not making light of compliance or daily operations skills. If you are missing either, special education in your school district will be chaotic. I am saying that those elements are not the ultimate goal for special education. Our ultimate goal is to increase student learning. That can only happen if we improve instruction. If all of our efforts focus on compliance activities and daily operations, we are not providing the leadership that we should.

How can you objectively determine the focus area of your own special education department? Ask principals and assistant principals. Send a survey with one question: "What are the top priorities for our district's central office special education department?" In many places, I'm afraid that the answers will be lacking. For example, "Write compliant IEPs," "Meet all timelines," "Ensure that we don't over-suspend students with disabilities," "Make sure our special education teachers are appropriately certified."

All of those things are important, but they are not our top priority. If the principals and assistant principals don't answer that the special education department prioritizes "Improving student learning by implementing effective, specially designed instruction," you have some work to do.

As special education administrators, we have to put a stake in the ground. We have to change the focus of our special education programs. We have to make improving instruction our top priority. There is an old saying that you can tell a person's priorities by looking at their checking account. How he spends his money reflects his priorities. A modification of that sentiment applies to the special education department. How you spend your time and attention reflects your priorities. What you talk about, train on, and monitor reflect what you expect your schools to focus on. If your schools think that special education is primarily focused on compliance and daily operation activities because that is what you have espoused, you must make changes. You want your work to be reflected by the following graphic:

Guiding Questions

* What is your special education department's main priority? What are your main messages? You can base this answer on the results of a survey or on how much time and attention you give to various main topics. Do the main messages focus on compliance activities, daily operations, or instruction? Explain your answer.

* As a special education leader, are you more comfortable leading compliance and daily operations activities across the school district or being an instructional leader? Why?

* If you are less comfortable leading instructional change efforts, what steps will you take to gain strength in the areas of instructional pedagogy and leadership?

Altering Your Focus, Beliefs, and Actions

I have come to realize that beliefs and actions are always aligned. In our personal and professional lives, we always act in accordance with our beliefs. What we actually do is aligned with what we believe. What is not always aligned is what we *say* we believe and what we actually believe. If you want to know what someone believes, don't listen to what they say, observe what they do.

This has a great relevance to your work as a special education director. If you say that providing GREAT instruction and specially designed instruction are the most powerful elements in your schools, but you don't back that up with actions, then your words don't really match your beliefs.

If all of your discussions, trainings, meetings, and interactions in your workday evolve around special education compliance and daily operations, you are clearly sending the message that you believe that those things are the most important things. Even if you say on occasion that instruction is the top priority, your actions are sending a much different and more truthful message about your beliefs.

Before you lead your district in a new direction about instruction for students with disabilities, it is critical to spend some time truly and honestly reflecting on your own beliefs. At your core, what is your top priority for your students? What do you truly value most when leading the district-wide special education program? In your mind, what are the most important things that you want to see for each and every child with a disability in your school district? If your answer centers around compliance and daily operations, then so be it. Keep moving in that direction.

If, on the other hand, you absolutely know in your heart that ultimately the instruction we provide for students is a life changer, then the rest of this book is for you. Even if you don't yet have the skillfulness or knowledge you need to make that happen, you can learn. You can lead your central office team, school principals, and all teachers to a place where they have the internal locus of control and the practices to make a difference for students through better instruction. You can do this. But you first must do the hard work of some serious and honest self-reflection. Do you truly believe in the importance of instruction?

Guiding Questions

- As a professional, what do you truly believe are the most important elements that must be provided to students with disabilities in your schools?

- Do your daily actions currently reflect those beliefs? If not, are you willing to change?

Altering Your Focus Through Special Education Leaders

School districts across the country vary greatly in size. Some school districts have thousands and thousands students with disabilities while other districts have dozens. The special education departments in these school districts obviously differ greatly. In some small districts, the special education director is the only central office special education employee and also wears many other hats. In the larger school districts, the special education department includes many, many professionals.

Regardless of the size, organization, or titles used in your district, you must have someone in the special education department who is adamantly focused on improving *instruction* for students with disabilities. To quote an old saying, he or she must be a "dog with a bone."

When your special education central office team discusses IEP training, he needs to ask how the training will include better instructional practices. When your team discusses meeting eligibility timelines, he should question how your district is impacting student learning. When you plan your training activities with principals and assistant principals, he must demand that the agenda includes implementing GREAT instruction for students with disabilities. You must give this person permission to be the tireless advocate for focusing on instruction, no matter the topic of conversation.

> How can you objectively determine the focus area of your own special education department? Ask principals and assistant principals. Send a survey with one question. "What are the top priorities for our district's central office special education department?"

This person must also have deep relationships with the curriculum and instruction department. He needs to have an impact on the various instructional initiatives as they are rolled out and supported across the district. (More on that later.)

If you are going to ask someone on your team to take on the role of being the powerful advocate for instruction, you must hire the right person. You must develop a job description that is focused on leading GREAT instruction across the district. Hiring a person who only has strong skills in compliance and daily operations will not suffice. They must have expertise in instruction.

In fact, perhaps we should turn our thinking upside down. Instead of having the special education director focus on daily operations and compliance activities, and hiring an expert in instruction, perhaps the special education director should have expertise in GREAT instruction for students with disabilities. That would definitely help transform the special education department.

Perhaps the director, with a profound knowledge of GREAT instruction, delegates compliance and daily operations activities and maintains the role of tireless instructional advocate. To be honest, the director will need knowledge in those two other areas, but her main mission can include focusing on improving instruction for your students.

Guiding Questions

- Is there someone in the special education department who is diligently and adamantly focused on instruction and turns almost every conversation into how instruction can be improved in order to impact student achievement? Have you given that person the charge and the power to lead this work?

- If not, will the instructional leader be the special education director or someone else in your department?

- How will you move your actions or the actions of one of your team members in that direction? As the leader, how will you set the expectation that this occurs and foster this focus on impacting instruction?

Altering Your Focus and Expecting Resistance

You will undoubtedly get pushback. In fact, most of your resistance might come from existing special education leaders in your district. I have had the great pleasure of working in multiple school districts in order to significantly improve the instruction provided to students with disabilities. The greatest resisters typically come from the central office special education team. You will definitely hear that they don't have time to focus on instruction. They will say they will get to that, or hope to get to that, after all of the compliance and daily operations activities are completed. Unfortunately, that will never happen. You might even hear, "Have you ever sat in a due process hearing? If we don't complete all of these things, we will end up there!"

Let's address that concern head-on. If your district has solid compliance and daily operations activities and you continually find yourself in heated IEP meetings that includes attorneys who represent the district and the child's family, then your issue may be instruction.

In my experiences, the overwhelming majority of parents of students with disabilities who are angry with the school or district have that perspective because of one of two things: they think their child is not progressing sufficiently or, in their mind, an employee with the school or district did something that angered them. There are certainly exceptions to that rule, but I have found it accurate in most cases.

In order to address the former, you must impact instruction. If you are a parent yourself, you can understand the heartbreak of having a child with an emotional/behavioral disorder or a specific learning disability, for example, and being unable to help make them successful either in their behavioral development or in their academic progress. It is understandable that the parent would have the perspective that the school should have the answers. I get that.

If you can't say that the student has received and is getting research-based universal instruction along with specially designed instruction in your school district, then there is progress that can be made instructionally. That is a different question than "Does the student have outstanding teachers?" He or she may, but does that mean the universal and specially designed instruction is consistently and routinely research-based and delivered with fidelity?

Being in those tense IEP meetings is certainly not easy. The stress can be overwhelming for everyone involved. Each one of those situations is quite unique and certainly takes an inordinate amount of time and energy. I am saying that if you find yourself continually in that situation and you have solid compliance and daily operations, then your next step as a special education administrator is to become a change agent regarding instruction. The first step is to change your focus regardless of the pushback that you face, especially from other administrators who want to focus exclusively on compliance and daily operations activities.

If you are the special education director in your school district, you must have the internal fortitude to set a new course and expect your team to do the same. Yes, you will have some staff members who continue to complete compliance and daily operations activities. That is still important. But improving instruction must be everyone's job. A profound focus on meeting the instructional needs of students must shape all of the work.

When I lead re-thinking and transformative work, I give some time for others to come along to the new vision. But I don't give them too long. In my experience, if a member of your team does not buy-in to nor own the new vision by January of the new school year in which you are providing this leadership, then they probably won't ever be fully supportive and engaged in this work. They don't have to have all of the skills necessary to impact instruction across the district, but they have to join the mindset that implementing GREAT instruction is the top priority. If you are having the same conversation repeatedly with select staff members about how you need to focus on instructional improvement and increasing student learning, you may have to make some difficult personnel choices.

Guiding Questions

- How will you lead the special education department to have a main focus on impacting instruction for students with disabilities? How will you foster, encourage, and lead this shift?

- How will you respond when members of your team ask good and probing questions about the direction for the department? What are your major points that can help develop your team?

- How many months will you give your staff to make this shift toward an instructional focus? What will occur if some personnel do not make that shift in the expected time frame?

X
Step 2: Know and Share the Data

In the first step, we discussed re-shaping the priorities and actions of the central office special education department. Now, we have to start thinking about how you influence others. The special education department will never be able to ensure GREAT instruction across every school if you work in isolation. In order to gain the attention of others and initiate some momentum, you need to know and share the data. Nothing speaks to others in our current context of educational accountability like data.

The No Child Left Behind legislation (2001) certainly had some shortcomings, but it was also very powerful in a few ways. Most notably, the legislation placed students with disabilities in the forefront. Before that time, students with disabilities were often not included in the statewide accountability system.

It may be hard for some of our younger colleagues to realize that before NCLB, many students with disabilities were not included in annual state-mandated assessments. If they were included, their answer documents were coded so that their scores were not calculated in the school-wide results. In essence, students with disabilities did not factor in how schools and districts were evaluated.

That changed dramatically with the reauthorization of the Elementary and Secondary Education Act (ESEA), also known as No Child Left Behind. With the new legislation, all students with disabilities were required to participate in the assessment system and their performance was included in the accountability matrix. (A very small percentage of students with disabilities, those with the most significant cognitive disabilities, took alternate assessments.)

Not only did the achievement of our students with disabilities count in the overall "grading" system for schools, they were one of the specific subgroups of students who were counted in isolation. In fact, several subgroups were named, including various racial and ethnic groups, students with disabilities, students deemed economically disadvantaged, and students who were English language learners (ELLs).

In order for a school and district to meet annual accountability standards, each of those subgroups had to make Adequate Yearly Progress (AYP). All of a sudden, special education administrators, like you, became very, shall we say, "popular." Suddenly, your students counted. In a very real and meaningful way, the Elementary and Secondary Education Act transformed "your students" into "our students."

I have always had the great pleasure of working with many dedicated and strong educators. Even before NCLB was implemented, those great teachers and administrators cared deeply about students with disabilities. They cared with their hearts. After the new accountability systems were put in place, everyone had to care with their brains.

In fact, students with disabilities weighed more statistically than virtually any other group of students when calculating whether or not a school or district met

Adequate Yearly Progress. You see, if a youngster named Micah had a learning disability and qualified for special education services, his performance influenced the statistical measurements of progress in several ways. Micah belonged to the "all" group, to his racial or ethnic subgroup, and to the disability subgroup. Micah might also have belonged to the economically disadvantaged and English language learners subgroups as well, depending on his individual needs.

As a member of the "all" group, Micah might have counted as one student out of 500 total students in the group. As part of his race or ethnic group, Micah might have counted as one student out of 250 or so, depending on the demographic representation of the student body. But as a member of the disability group, Micah counted as one of only 50 students, so his progress accounts for a whopping 2% of the performance for the entire disability group overall—a substantial influence. Yes, Micah's progress or lack of progress had a far greater influence on whether or not a school met Adequate Yearly Progress than many other students. Statistically, Micah weighed seemingly exponentially more than a student who did not have a disability and may have been only in two larger groups.

Again, as special education administrators, we became very popular along with our students. Instead of receiving the last batch of textbooks when they arrived (if they arrived at all), lots of school administrators lobbied to ensure that we had the instructional materials we needed. Instead of being an afterthought during important instructional initiatives, our students were suddenly at the center of the conversation.

The No Child Left Behind legislation has been reauthorized and is now called the Every Student Succeeds Act (ESSA) (2015). For the most part, accountability systems will be designed by the state departments of education, but the importance of the disability subgroup will remain. Our students with disabilities will continue to be a prominent component of the accountability systems across the country. In fact, that is always going to be the case, regardless of how many times the federal or state accountability systems change. Moving forward, our students will always count. That is a good thing.

Because of the disability group's influence on a school and the district's ability to meet accountability standards, we must share the data that reflect our students' progress and their impact. By sharing the data, we can create momentum so that educators and leaders throughout your school district see the value of increasing the achievement of all students, especially students with disabilities. We can create the leverage so that improving instruction for students with disabilities becomes everyone's job.

> In order to gain the attention of others and to initiate some momentum, you need to know and share the data. Nothing speaks to others in our current context of educational accountability like data.

Understand the Accountability System

If you are going to create a common sense of urgency that permeates the central office and schools, you have to speak the language that others are paying attention to—the statewide accountability system. Therefore, you have to know the system deeply.

If your state's accountability system includes a 100-point scale, you need to have a deep understanding of how each of those potential points are earned or not earned. If your state's accountability system provides grades to each school and district, you need to understand each variable that feeds into that A through F rating system. It is insufficient to have a *general* understanding of your state's accountability system; you must understand each of the variables and how the different elements are actually calculated.

Make a List of Every Category Impacted by Students with Disabilities

After you have a deep understanding of your state's accountability system, it is best to determine how the performance of students with disabilities impacts each element. Make a list of all the components that include students with disabilities.

First of all, any "all" category will naturally include students with disabilities. If your state's accountability system includes "all" categories for discipline infractions or absences, students with disabilities influence those calculations as well. In fact, for any category that attempts to measure the progress of students sorted according to academic performance, behavior, or attendance, students with disabilities likely have a profound impact on those calculations because many students with disabilities struggle to meet grade-level standards and sometimes exhibit a higher frequency of disciplinary suspensions. And, for a variety of reasons, students with disabilities are sometimes at a greater risk of missing school.

Next, students with disabilities will be represented in different subgroups as well. Every student has a race or ethnicity. Across the country, students with disabilities generally represent approximately 8-9% of the entire student population (U.S. Department of Education, 2015). It is helpful to know the percentage of students in the various subgroups who have disabilities. Out of the Hispanic, White, African American, and American Indian subgroups, for example, what percentage of those students have disabilities? Of the economically disadvantaged and English language learners subgroups, how many students, or what percentage of students, qualify for special education?

This helps you in two ways. First, you now have a clearer perception of how students with disabilities impact the performance of each of the subgroups. Second, you can also detect any troubling patterns. If students with disabilities account for more than 9% of any "all" group or subgroup, for example, then you might be over-identifying students with special needs.

In addition to the "all" group and the different subgroups, your students with disabilities might impact other categories as well. In some states, for example, the accountability system includes a "gap" metric. The metric might measure the progress of the lowest 25% of learners and whether or not they are closing the gap with more typical learners. If a school or district is able to move their lowest performing quartile drastically closer to the state's mean score, for example, then they are rewarded with earning more points in the "gap" category. On the other hand, if the lowest quartile continues to lag behind or loses ground to the state's 50th percentile, then the school or district earns fewer points or no points at all.

Students with disabilities, as you might imagine, constitute a large percentage of the lowest 25% of performers. Therefore, they have a significant influence on the points earned in that category. If you can explain the importance students with disabilities have on that data element, and all others, then you can help create a sense of urgency across your district.

Do you see the potential for sharing the data? If special education departments can be astute at demonstrating the disability subgroup is critical to ensuring that schools or districts score well on the statewide accountability system, then other leaders and teachers will be on board to move the needle forward in providing GREAT instruction for all students, including those students with disabilities.

Hints About Displaying Data

There is a fine line between data analysis and data paralysis. Every effective data presentation always generates additional questions. What would the data tell us if we disaggregated by gender? By specific disability? By overage and underage students for their respective grade level? These additional questions can go on and on.

We have to analyze the data to an appropriate depth. We have to sift the data so that they reveal a clear and decisive direction for our proposed next steps. We want our data analyses to be purposeful. All too often, we become so inundated with data that our analyses begin to obscure the best and clearest course of action. That obscurity is data paralysis.

If you are going to be effective at garnering deep partnerships and developing a cross-departmental team that is committed to assisting students with disabilities, then you must know the data and you must share that data with precision and appropriate messaging. You want enough data to inspire action, but not so much data that your colleagues' eyes begin to glaze over. Here are a few suggestions to consider whenever presenting data:

- **Limit the numerical data in any presentation to no more than seven or so slides or graphics.**
- **Use the same data view throughout those slides.** For example, if your data are best presented with trend lines, then use trend lines throughout the presentation. If you first present data as ratios, use ratios for all successive

slides. This consistency allows your audience to formulate relationships between one data element and the next, instead of trying to grasp the math behind each individual slide.

- **Use the data to tell stories about boys and girls.** If you are discussing graduation rates for students with disabilities, show a picture of 10 students' faces. If your graduation rate for students with disabilities is 60%, cover the faces of four of those students. Or, show photos of students with disabilities in your district who have overcome great odds (with the appropriate confidentiality releases, of course). At the end of the day, our work is all about our students. Use their photos and stories to demonstrate that.
- **Use comparison points.** If 70% of the students with disabilities pass the end-of-course test in geometry, the audience does not know if that is a high or low percentage. Compare that data to the statewide data or to districts of comparable size and demographics. That comparison will provide a relational point of reference.
- **Use trend lines.** Single data points tell you very little. Show your district's or school's trend line in comparison to the state's or comparison districts' trend lines. If your district or school is below the comparison point, but has closed that gap drastically over the last four years, then you should stay on the same path. If, however, the district is below the comparison for the first time with a few years of declining performance, then the next steps actions are very different. The trends tell the story.

In addition, you should plan multiple sessions to analyze data. Adults need time to process data. At initial presentations, you should provide one set of data. At subsequent presentations, you can dig deeper and facilitate more sophisticated discussions.

Some of my emphasis on data might sound manipulative, or too obsessed with numerical information or the accountability system in your state. That is certainly not my intent. At my core, I know that the overwhelming majority of educators are extremely dedicated to their students—all of their students. They work tirelessly to provide an outstanding education for their youngsters.

They are inundated with initiatives, messages, priorities, and the never-ending needs of students and staff. As you know, education is a hard job, but it is enormously rewarding and noble. Due to the constant "noise," it can be extremely difficult to have and maintain a clear focus. At no fault of their own, it is entirely possible for educators to work endless hours without achieving the optimum efficiency needed to have the greatest impact on the greatest number of students.

That is where you come in. You have to help provide focus. If you can clearly demonstrate the needs of all students, including students with disabilities, with hard data, then you can help bring clarity and focus to the work. If you can explain the accountability system, the district's strengths and weaknesses, and how the performance of students with disabilities can be enormously impacted through

GREAT instruction, then you can help provide a path toward higher achievement, not only for students with disabilities but for many other students as well.

Additional Notes About Data

Please also remember that there are multiple types of district data. There are summative components that usually include annual statewide assessment data. That is the equivalent of conducting an autopsy. It is after the fact. Perhaps more importantly, there are formative or leading data. This might include the results of the district-wide benchmarks that are administered every six weeks. With the data, you can make mid-course corrections to instructional initiatives.

In addition to student outcome data, there are adult practice data. Things like formal or informal observations and the review of artifacts. In my current position, I supervise the district's RTI (or MTSS) work. Each school maintains a log of students who are participating in different tiers of interventions. Every school's log must include each participating student's: 1) Area of Weakness, 2) Research-based Intervention, and 3) Validated Progress Monitoring Tool. In addition, each student must have a file that includes his or her trend line data from the progress monitoring tool and documentation that indicates that an ongoing analysis of data took place.

By looking at a single log from a school, I can determine if there are instructional misperceptions. Often, a log includes a student's weakness as reading comprehension, but the intervention and progress monitoring tool that were documented for the child do not match that area of weakness. I can also see if the seventh-grade teachers tend to default to a particular area of weakness for most children before analyzing each student's individual needs. With well-designed artifacts, you can gain real insight into adult practices.

Lastly, you must realize that quantitative analysis of student data is only the first step. Once you get everyone's attention with the data, you have to facilitate others as they try to determine why the data look like they do—both good and bad. Determining the "why" will help the team determine the next steps.

Guiding Questions

- In your school district, can you put your hands on a current and comprehensive data report for the performance of students with disabilities, including trend lines over time? If not, how can you work with your team to complete one?

- If a data report is current and available, and you have determined "what" it tells you, has your team taken the next step to determine the "why" behind the data?

- If you have a current and available data report, and you have completed the "what" and "why," what are the priority goals and actions currently in place to improve student achievement? If the data report is not used to set priorities, analyze the data to determine the district's strengths and weaknesses for students with disabilities.

- Do the special education leaders have a deep and thorough understanding of the state's accountability system and the impact that students with disabilities are having on your district's and schools' annual accountability report? If so, describe that impact.

- Have you shared that data report and analysis with different departments in the central office, principals, and teachers across your school district? If so, describe how.

XI
Step 3: Know What It Takes to Change Teacher Practices

So far, we have discussed the first two steps for special education departments to ultimately assist in making GREAT instruction occur across every school in your district. These two steps have covered the skills and focus needed by your central office team.

Now we are going to jump forward and start thinking with the end in mind. Let's do some backward planning. If we want to see GREAT instruction in every class, we have to impact the practices of our teachers. They are the ones doing the most important work in our districts. They are providing instruction.

In order to increase student learning, we have to help shape teacher practices. It may sound like I am placing all of the responsibility for instruction on our teachers' shoulders. I am not. As leaders, we have a tremendous responsibility to provide the support, training, environment, and context where teachers can deliver that instruction. We must do our part.

The million-dollar question is, "How do we change teacher's practices?" Think for a minute about the various initiatives that you have seen come and go. In the field of education, we have seen initiative after initiative, silver bullet after silver bullet travel through our schools. They are unveiled with great fanfare, last a few years (if that), then ultimately fade away.

Some of those initiatives have actually included strong research-based practices, while others included the latest educational fad. At the end of the day, however, most of these initiatives did not meaningfully impact the practices of our teachers and leaders. In our country, we are extremely ineffective at changing our schools so that we actually see differences in our classrooms. So let's dig into the question of changing teacher practices. To clear our heads, we are going to step out of the public school arena. Let's review another context to discuss changing adult practices.

Think about your nearest martial arts studio. Elisha is interested in taking martial arts classes. In fact, she has decided to dedicate herself to earning a black belt. She was athletic in high school but became less active as she grew older. Elisha not only sets her sights on earning a black belt, but also sets a timeline for gaining that recognition of her skills. She sets an ambitious goal of earning that black belt in two years. What does she need to do to improve her skills so that she will steadily grow as a martial artist, ultimately earning a black belt in the next 24 months?

The obvious answer is Elisha needs practice—lots of it. But she needs other elements also. She needs to find a martial arts studio whose coaches have a history of effectively training adults to become black belts. By finding a studio with that history, she will be sure she participates in an "evidenced-based" curriculum, proven effective in assisting the participants in reaching their goals.

It will not serve Elisha's purpose to sign up with a martial arts studio that primarily focuses on five- and six-year-old potential martial artists who quickly lose interest in the sport. She needs to be trained by professionals who have established a pattern of assisting adult athletes in acquiring their black belts.

By enrolling in an established, effective martial arts studio, she can be sure her coach has a clear vision of the end goal. The coach will know specifically what skills Elisha needs to develop in order to earn a black belt. She has to become adept at performing specific kicks and punches. She needs to complete predetermined sequences of martial arts movements that combine to make a whole. She needs competence in sparring. Her coach must have a clear and very specific understanding of what Elisha will need to learn and the skills she will need to perfect over the next two years. As Elisha moves through this process, her understanding of those black belt competencies will also become clear and concrete.

In collaboration with her coach, Elisha also needs to determine her starting point. Together, they need to determine her strengths and weaknesses near the onset of her quest. They will determine where she stands on elements like flexibility, stamina, strength, and coordination. Based on this analysis, her instructor will undoubtedly try to capitalize on her areas of strength while improving her areas of weakness.

> If we want to see GREAT instruction in every class, we have to impact the practices of our teachers. They are the ones doing the most important work in our districts. They are providing instruction.

If she is extremely flexible but has poor balance, she will continue to stretch before every practice and will have a good range of motion in her kicks, but she will spend extra time and energy on honing her balance. This initial assessment will help determine the specific areas that will assist her in reaching her goals while outlining skill barriers that must be improved in order to move forward.

Elisha also needs an opportunity to practice multiple times each week and to receive systematic feedback from an expert—her coach. (Just as practice turns and feedback are critical for students in school, they are also critical for adults who are learning new skills.) She needs to follow the curriculum and receive suggestions, corrections, and encouragement on her efforts. If she is not putting her weight on the correct foot, her coach needs to point that out. If she is dropping her guarding arm, she needs to be reminded to focus on that arm. When she hits the bag with power or blocks a punch effectively, Elisha's coach needs to reinforce her correct technique. That systematic coaching will steadily enable Elisha to add and refine new skills on the way to her ultimate goal.

During that process, she will also need to reach benchmarks. Elisha's goal is to attain her black belt in two years. Along the way, she needs to know if she is on pace to meet that goal. The study of martial arts includes a system of benchmarking. Potential black belts are tested periodically to see if they can earn the next belt color.

She may go from a white belt to a yellow belt to a green belt and so on until she reaches a black belt. If she does not earn those various rankings in a specific time frame, she will not be on target to earn her black belt in two years. That monitoring of her progress will inform her workouts. If she is on target and earns those belts as expected, Elisha should stay the course. If she loses momentum and fails to stay on pace, she will need to accelerate her training activities to get back on track.

It is easy to assume that Elisa will learn all of her new skills from her coach. Relying on one person to meet those needs, however, is insufficient. Her time frame is very aggressive, so she will have to maximize her learning. Therefore, Elisha needs to surround herself with other people who are committed to martial arts. In all likelihood, these folks will be pursuing the same goal at the martial arts studio. Some of her peers will be more adept than she is and some will be less so. By participating with a cadre of similarly minded individuals, she will learn both formally and informally.

At times, she will receive explicit instruction from her peers. She may ask Thomas to show her how he keeps his balance when he is completing a kicking combination. At other times, she will informally notice that Maria is using her entire body when she punches and that seems to be an effective technique. Elisha will then incorporate those techniques into her own practice. A group of athletes that are working toward the same goal will all benefit from the brainstorming, modeling, motivation, and element of competition that is present in any athletic pursuit.

Notice that Elisha's circle of feedback is being enlarged. She is receiving feedback from her coaches and also from interaction with her peers. Again, the longer I work in the field of education, the more I realize that most learning is fostered through practice turns and feedback.

As Elisha's skillfulness develops, another source of feedback will develop as well. She will be her own source of feedback. She will recognize when her weight is on the wrong foot or when her power is limited by not torqueing her torso. She will give herself feedback and make those adjustments. This feedback is critical and necessary and develops over time. It should also be fostered so that she is self-reflective of her practices. Therefore, Elisha becomes more and more of a self-directed learner, an awareness we want to develop in our school-age youngsters. In the athletic arena, this self-directed feedback never replaces feedback from a coach, but it is critical to help Elisha develop into a master martial artist.

Elisha also needs one last critical component to reach her goal. She needs to ensure that all of the resources in her life are aligned. She needs to determine that earning a black belt is a major personal goal. This is not the time for her to pursue another college degree.

Elisha needs to recruit people in her life. As a wife and mother of three children, she needs to have some conversations with her husband and children to determine if this is a goal that the family can help her pursue. Are all of the people in her life aligned to help her achieve her goal? Will her husband and children support her in allocating her time differently?

In summary, it is obvious that in order to change her "practices" to reach her goal, Elisha will need some very specific components. Her needs will include the following:

- A clearly defined vision of her goal that is shared by her coach and herself. They need to know the specific skills that she will need in order to be considered a black belt.
- A needs assessment that determines her starting point in terms of her physical strengths and weaknesses as related to martial arts.
- Engagement in a proven curriculum.
- Lots of practice with ongoing feedback and coaching from an expert.
- Formative assessments that will provide information so she and her coach can refine her training toward her end goal.
- Participation in a group of peers who are pursuing the same goal in order to formally and informally learn from and motivate one another.
- The opportunity to self-reflect and to become more skillful at giving herself feedback.
- Alignment of the people and resources in her life to ensure that they are all committed to helping her achieve her goal.

The original question was, "How do we impact the practices of our teachers?" It actually takes the same elements to change teachers' practices as it takes to change Elisha's skillfulness. (In fact, I would argue that it takes much more effort to become a magnificent teacher in two years than to become a black belt in that time.)

Teachers need a clearly defined end goal for what instruction should look like in their classrooms. They need to specifically understand the components of GREAT instruction, particularly for students with disabilities, and what those components will look like. They also need to practice those instructional techniques and receive ongoing coaching and feedback toward their efforts.

They need to review their progress with implementation against predesigned benchmarks. For teachers, that information not only determines whether their practices are improving over time but also whether students are showing increased achievement. If students are not learning, or if the teachers' instructional practices are not improving sufficiently, it is clear that the training and support provided to the educators must be improved to get both the teachers and students back on track.

Educators need to work with their colleagues, other teachers, and administrators who are working toward the same end goal of specific instructional improvements. They need to benefit from one another's experiences, expertise, brainstorming, and problem solving. They need to observe one another implementing GREAT instruction, not to judge or evaluate one another, but to learn. They need to be engaged in conversations about the instructional elements they are implementing and the effectiveness for student learning.

They also need to benefit from aligned resources. All of the personnel in the school and at the central office—particularly the leaders, instructional coaches, and external supporters—need to be aligned in working toward the same improvements in instruction. They all must have the same clear vision of what effective instruction should look like in every classroom. Any feedback that a teacher receives should be consistent regardless of the specific person providing the feedback. New information that is provided regarding other initiatives should be aligned to this work. School administrators, central office personnel, and instructional coaches must have carefully defined the critical elements to be seen so they are looking for the same observable practices. That way, the school will move efficiently toward the same, clear end goal.

How does this approach compare to the rollout of many initiatives in our school districts and schools? How does Elisha's plan compare to the experiences of our classroom teachers when new programs or priorities are unveiled? Unfortunately, most school districts and special education departments do not operate in this way. Central offices often work in silos where different priorities are sent to teachers from different personnel. Title I has their requirements as does the district's curriculum and instruction department, while the special education department and others promote a different set of priorities.

Teachers are inundated with misaligned priorities and are then asked to make some sense of the work. In addition, teachers are often offered one-shot training activities with little follow-up, support, coordinated brainstorming, or reflection to determine next steps as the instructional techniques are attempted and later refined.

Therefore, teachers are responsible for somehow pulling in the variety of expectations and the content of numerous misaligned professional development initiatives to build a cohesive instructional program. In the end, this scattered approach to improving teachers' practices and student achievement results in ineffective practices, or in a general disregard for all new initiatives. "This too shall pass," the teachers say to themselves.

As special education administrators, we must solve the problem of misaligned initiatives. If we are going to influence the achievement of students with disabilities, we have to help align the work toward improved instructional practices, but we certainly cannot do this alone, nor are we in a position to do so. In the following chapters, we will continue the list of these 10 steps to making this work happen consistently in your school district. Notice how so much of this work centers on developing deep partnerships so that this work is not isolated to the special education department, but is a top priority for all educators across the district.

The North Star of this work, however, must be a clear understanding of what it takes to improve teacher practices. We have to keep the illustration of Elisha and her martial arts efforts front and center. As special education administrators, we must help build an aligned and coordinated system of teacher support in order to impact students.

Guiding Questions

- In your school district, is the implementation of instructional initiatives more similar to Elisha's black belt initiative or to the misalignment of initiatives that often frustrate effective changes to teacher practices? Explain your answer.

- In your school district, is the work of the special education department aligned and in concert with the curriculum and instruction department, Title I, and other offices?

- Do teachers participate in ongoing training, support, and brainstorming regarding instructional priorities, or are teachers asked to participate in a variety of one-shot workshops with little follow-through and support? Describe examples to support your answer.

XII
Step 4: Sell It at the Central Office

As a special education administrator, you are in a unique position. You have a tremendous amount of responsibility that impacts virtually every classroom in your district, and yet you rarely have line-item authority over the principals and teachers who are implementing the special education programs. This holds equally true for the three buckets of the special education department: instruction, compliance, and daily operations. You are responsible for making it happen, but you don't necessarily have authority.

There is some good news that goes with this seemingly impossible job description. Authority isn't all it is cracked up to be. Most long-term, deep change does not occur because someone is forced or required to do it. Deep change is usually fostered through leaders who inspire, motivate, and influence the thinking and actions of others. So, the notion that everything would change for the better if only special education administrators were given the authority is a little farfetched. We have to be change agents, not chiefs.

Truth be told, however, we are limited in the leverage we have *unless* we create more leverage. Our voice alone will not result in the type of change that needs to occur. Therefore, we need more voices. Across the district, we must create a sweeping momentum for change that includes a wide variety of personnel that are aligned in their messaging, training, and activities. We must also develop a context in which that change can take root and be supported through the various stages of implementation.

Several years ago, the National Staff Development Council (now known as Learning Forward) developed standards for implementing adult change (Hirsh, 2007). The standards fell under three headings: context, content, and process. Even though their standards have been revised since their original formulation, those three categories still speak to me.

In order to change and impact the instructional practices of our teachers and school leaders, we must change the *context* in which folks do their work. We must also make sure that what we ask our colleagues to implement is research-based and will impact student achievement. That is the *content*. Lastly, we must provide the training, ongoing coaching, brainstorming, and collaborative work that teachers need so that new practices are attempted, debriefed, refined, and implemented with fidelity. Those ongoing support pieces (like Elisha's work with her coach and fellow athletes in the previous chapter) is the *process*. Let's continue discussing the context by developing deep partnerships with others in the central office.

The Leader for Curriculum and Instruction

You must engage with the person who leads the overall instructional program throughout the district. His or her title might be deputy superintendent of teaching and learning, director of curriculum and instruction, or something else. The title is not really important. You need to recognize who is charged with the overall umbrella of instruction for all students in your school district. You must learn deeply about his or her priorities and initiatives. You must understand the recent history of the instructional programs, including different initiatives, materials, and efforts that have been implemented. Then you need to bring some fresh insight to that work.

Many years ago, the special education department would lead instructional efforts for students with disabilities. The special education department would provide training to special education teachers and paraprofessionals while the "general education department" would provide training to everyone else. We wondered why we struggled to have a lasting impact on instructional practices across the district.

> Authority isn't all it is cracked up to be. Most long-term, deep change does not occur because someone is forced or required to do it. Deep change is usually fostered through leaders who inspire, motivate, and influence the thinking and actions of others.

In your district, if the special education department is providing isolated training to special education teachers (regarding students who are pursuing grade-level standards), you must stop. It is a waste of time, money, and effort. It makes no sense to provide classroom management, reading, mathematics, or, heaven forbid, co-teaching training to special education teachers in isolation. What can a special education teacher do with that training? Try to convince the rest of the school to implement those practices? If you are trying to impact instructional practices and student achievement with this isolated approach, the visual organizer below reflects your work.

DISTRICT-WIDE INSTRUCTIONAL INITIATIVES

SPECIAL EDUCATION INSTRUCTIONAL INITIATIVES

In essence, your work is isolated and will not ultimately improve the instruction seen in your classrooms. Remember that over 60% of students with disabilities across the country spend more than 80% of their school day in general education settings (U.S. Department of Education, 2014). If we are going to impact the instruction provided to our students and other students, we have to impact the larger circle. Many of our students with disabilities spend many of their instructional periods in general education classes with only one teacher—a general education teacher. During other periods, our students are participating in classes with co-teachers—a general and special education teacher. In either of those scenarios, you cannot improve instruction without impacting the practices of general education teachers. Again, isolated training regarding instruction for students with disabilities (who are pursuing grade-level achievement standards) will not work. You have to impact the entire field of general, core instruction starting with the leader of curriculum and instruction.

We cannot create separate silos of improvement. We must enlarge the other, more powerful circle so that it is responsive to our students and their needs, as supported by all teachers—general education and special education personnel.

In the first half of the book, a list of specific instructional practices was offered as the foundation for specially designed instruction. You might notice that every one of those instructional practices will benefit many students who do not have an IEP. Every one of those practices can certainly be beneficial to students who struggle but are not eligible for special education. In fact, many of those instructional practices can be beneficial for *every* student.

Therefore, one of your critical efforts must be to develop a deep partnership with the leader of the curriculum and instruction department, regardless of the title of that department in your district. You must suggest that the list of instructional practices could be high-level practices in all classrooms, for all children.

Ultimately, you must influence the direction and message that is provided by that department. You want that group of leaders to enlarge their initiatives so that they are beneficial for all students, including students with disabilities. You want their work, informed by your support and insight, to be reflected by the graphic below.

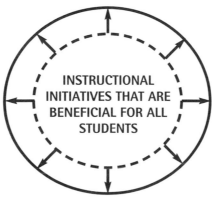

Principal Supervisors

You must also develop deep partnerships with the professional(s) who supervise school principals. Those individuals help establish the priorities for their assigned schools. They provide ongoing support, training, brainstorming, and problem solving for principals.

You must become their best friend. You need to become embedded and enlarge the instructional improvements that they are supporting in their schools. That will include responding to their needs and determining how to provide support. The special education director and the entire department should be trusted and respected so much that your insights are considered important and valuable. Therefore, when you offer the instructional practices that define the foundation for specially designed instruction in your district, the principal supervisors will listen. They will see how those instructional practices will have a strong and positive impact on the achievement of students with disabilities, other students who struggle, and students who are performing quite well.

Other Central Office Departments

You also need to develop partnerships with other departments, namely the budget office and the department that analyzes and publishes data. In most school districts, the draft budget is proposed to the board of education in February or so for the following school year. It is then shared with the public for a period of time in which the board and the public have a chance to review it. After at least a month, the board takes the budget up for a vote. In some places, the board only votes on state and local dollars. In other places, federal dollars are also approved by the board.

Either way, the special education program in your district is supported by federal, state, and local dollars. It is extremely beneficial to have a strong collaborative partnership with the central office personnel who develop the district-wide budgets. The federal IDEA budgets only cover a small portion of the funds that it takes to educate children with disabilities in your district or any other district. Therefore, there are many decisions made regarding other funds that impact the instruction that is provided to your students.

The individuals who crunch data are also extremely important. Over the last several years, federal and state laws, rules, and regulations have clearly become focused on accountability. Schools and school districts are evaluated or graded based in large part on increases and/or performance of all students, including students with disabilities. As special education administrators, we need a deep understanding of the accountability processes and data (as mentioned in a previous chapter). The folks who usually have that knowledge are the folks who crunch and submit data to the state department of education. They not only understand the intricacies of the accountability system but also possess the expertise involved in pulling specific data sets regarding the performance of students with disabilities. They can help you determine the mathematical impact that students with disabilities are having on your district's and school's annual results, a leverage point that is extremely valuable.

Perhaps more important, data personnel can provide data that reflects how students are making progress throughout the school year. That information can help principals, teachers and your department make mid-course adjustments to the instruction that is being provided, thereby accelerating learning during the current school year.

Office Space

Now is a pretty good time to discuss office space. In many districts, especially somewhat larger districts, the central office special education offices are in a different building or a special wing of the main office. This is a problem. The special education department must be fully integrated and a critical component of the overall instructional work in the district. If we are housed in a different location than the rest of the curriculum and instruction department, our ability to collaborate is limited. In fact, we want more than collaboration. We want true partnership and to be embedded in the overall work. We want to be part of the team, not a visitor.

Through my years working in educational leadership, I have learned that most decisions don't occur in meetings. Yes, we have staff meetings and cross-curricular meetings. We plan brainstorming sessions and set aside time to problem solve and plan. But most decisions are not made during those scheduled times.

Most decisions are made in hallways, at the coffee machine, or when one staff member drops into a colleague's office with an idea. Many, perhaps most, administrators never realize the importance of this informal contact. They often spend hours preparing a proposal with all of the bells and whistles, major goals, outlines, and budget items for the pending staff meeting.

They are disappointed when the meeting agenda is packed and their ideas are barely reviewed. Their plans, even great ones, are not truly considered.

If you want to have an impact on your colleagues' perspectives and actions regarding educating students with disabilities, and you want to truly hear and learn from their expertise, then many, many conversations must happen daily, over extended periods of time. All of those informal conversations slowly shape their (and your) thinking, thereby fertilizing the ground for the implementation of initiatives.

That cannot happen easily if the special education offices are isolated from

> **Through my years working in educational leadership, I have learned that most decisions don't occur in meetings. Yes, we have staff meetings and cross-curricular meetings. We plan brainstorming sessions and set aside time to problem solve and plan. But most decisions are not made during those scheduled times.**

the daily work of the instruction department. If your office space is currently separated, work toward getting that changed. Or if your district is considering separating the offices because of the availability of potential new office space, try to stop it.

Having larger offices with better facilities might sound positive, but if that includes separating special education from the other departments, then the overall instructional message will only become more fractured with schools, principals, and teachers hearing separated silos of information.

If your offices are currently separated and there is not an immediate opportunity to change that, you are going to have to work extra hard to become embedded in order to impact the overall instructional program. You must create situations where you and your team are available for all of those informal conversations. I would even go so far as staking out conference rooms and extra cubicles for an extension office. "Do you mind if some members of my team and I work in these areas a few days a week?" That way, your daily presence will become known and the voice for students with disabilities will become a seamless part of the conversation.

Guiding Questions

- Is the special education central office team fully embedded in the overall work of instruction across the district? Explain your answer.

- Does your department have ongoing partnerships and collaboration with the curriculum and instruction department? Is the work of your department truly embedded in the larger work of instructional leadership? Provide examples that support your answer.

- Does your department have true partnerships with those professionals who supervise principals that go beyond solving a particular issue in a school? Provide examples to support your answer.

- Is there an ongoing collaboration with budget and data personnel? How are those partnerships demonstrated?

- Does the special education central office team have continuous, informal interactions with the members of the curriculum and instruction department? Is everyone part of one large team?

- If you have a need to broaden and deepen true partnerships with other leaders in the central office, how can you do that on a daily basis (beyond the regularly scheduled meetings)?

XIII
Steps 5, 6, and 7:
Be Strategic

Step 5: Focus on Instructional Practices That Impact All Students, Not Just Students with Disabilities

This message has been embedded throughout this book, but it bears repeating and emphasizing: The instructional practices that I have offered as the foundation of specially designed instruction are beneficial to a wide variety of students, not just students with disabilities.

If you decide to select from my list or build your own list of instructional practices, choose those practices that are not only needed by students with disabilities, but are needed by other students. Increasing practice turns and feedback, for example, is good for every student in the classroom. Likewise, implementing research-based vocabulary instruction is beneficial for every student.

You will have a much easier time convincing your central office colleagues, principals, and teachers to implement your foundational list of specially designed instruction if they immediately see how they will benefit many students in their classrooms. You are not only providing them the data that indicate the impact that students with disabilities are having on overall student achievement (as defined by the state's accountability system), you are providing a solution that will assist the youngsters with disabilities and many other students.

Step 6: Only Focus on One to Three Instructional Practices a Year

In the visual organizer, there are several instructional practices that fall under the general heading of Specially Designed Instruction. Some of those practices can be applied to all content areas while some are specific to mathematics. In addition, within the area of universal, Tier 1 instruction, there are several things that might be addressed. Lastly, all of the practices will need to be implemented in all classes, including co-teaching classes in which both teachers should be routinely implementing small group instruction at the same time (in addition to student independent groups that might be occurring).

Needless to say, you can't implement all of those elements in one school year. The visual organizer from the first half of the book is a multi-year outline. You are going to have to make some choices and prioritize for the first year of implementation. If you ask educators to implement all of those things, even if you have great partnerships and alignment with the other departments in the central office, you will overwhelm everyone. Folks will push back or completely ignore this work.

In your district, you need to choose one to three instructional practices for next year's implementation. How do you choose? You want to pick those instructional practices that have the greatest chance of being successful. If this is your first year of really focusing on instruction in this way, you want quick wins. You want victories and movement. Don't pick those things that will result in great resistance and frustration. Let's get some fast victories. From my vantage point, I can't tell you which practices will be the most strategic in your school district. It is all based on your context. I can, however, provide some considerations that might be helpful.

Consideration #1: Let the data drive you. You have completed a thorough analysis of the achievement data for students with disabilities. In addition, either you or others have completed data analyses regarding the achievement trends for all students. Let those two hubs of data help you determine which instructional practices, when applied in all classrooms, will have the greatest impact for all students, including students with disabilities. In addition, think about the next two considerations.

Consideration #2: In your district, do you have a low percentage of students with disabilities who are educated in general education classrooms? Across the country, roughly 62% of students with disabilities spend at least 80% of their instructional day in general education classrooms (U.S. Department of Education, 2014). If that percentage is in the 40s or low 50s in your district, that is probably your first place to start. Focus on increasing the number of co-teaching classes that are available so that more students with disabilities can be supported in those classes. Make it a priority to focus on small-group instruction in those classes and to use some of the other practices (i.e., drastically increasing practice turns and feedback). Remember, if you make a significant movement in inclusive efforts to reach at least the national average, you will get a bump in student achievement. Unfortunately, you will see a plateau if you don't impact the instructional practices in those classes, so you must diligently focus on instruction also.

Consideration #3: Is the curriculum and instruction department focusing on one or more specific instructional practices that lend themselves to this work? If, for example, they are prioritizing effective vocabulary instruction, help them expand that initiative so that it is impactful for all students, including students with disabilities. That department may be focusing on effective feedback. Help them build in drastically increasing student practice turns along with that feedback. The point is to use the existing initiatives and momentum to impact your students who have IEPs.

Step 7: Partner, Train, Support, and Brainstorm with Principals and Assistant Principals Often

You must partner deeply with principals. They are critical professionals. They have the enormous responsibility for leading their schools so that all students reach higher levels of achievement through effective instruction. They also have tons of other responsibilities. In essence, they are the equivalent of the mayor of a small town. They have to consider safety, daily operations, traffic patterns (in the hallways and parking lot), transportation, food service, and layers of employees. The list goes on and on.

Oftentimes, special education administrators get frustrated when a middle-of-the-road special education issue does not ride to the top of the list for a school principal. It is certainly not because principals don't care. They do. They care deeply. Most times, their inaction just reflects the magnitude of their job and the flood of communication that comes their way.

As special education leaders, we have to try our best to see the work through their eyes. Instead of trying to have them focus on those things that are priorities in the special education department, we must determine their priorities and see how we can support them in their work.

That is not to say we abandon everything that we know is needed regarding special education. We have specialized knowledge and expertise regarding the instruction needed for our students. We also have deep and thorough knowledge about the compliance requirements that apply to our youngsters. You need to continue with that work.

I am asking you to shape your work so that it speaks to and is responsive to principals, not just for a relatively few students who have disabilities, but for many students who could benefit from the instructional elements you are promoting. Instead of being isolated—an additional silo which principals have to consider—provide solutions that meet their needs to educate all of their students. Show them data in a unique way to provide a fresh perspective. That data should not only include students with disabilities, but perhaps data for all students or data regarding students who struggle but do not have a disability.

Through the years, I have worked with a variety of personnel who support one or two schools' special education programs. Their titles have varied: lead teacher for special education, special education lead teacher, and so on. Regardless of the title, I keep the same message. In their role, they must provide great insight and support. They have to be change agents who contribute greatly and help expand the priorities of the school so that all students can be successful. I know that those personnel are meeting that challenge when the principal insists that they are a part of the school's leadership team.

The principal should value the contributions of that individual so much that he or she should say, "We have to schedule our leadership team meetings on the days that Ms. Jones is assigned to our school. Her contributions are needed." Once that person is part of the school's leadership team, he or she can help shape the work so that it includes the needs of students with disabilities. His or her influence has to enlarge the instructional initiatives and priorities so that all students can be successful.

Train Principals Often

School districts usually have monthly or bimonthly meetings where all principals gather. If you are the special education director, you want to get on that agenda as frequently as possible. You want to provide engaging, collaborative, hands-on, participatory training to principals regularly so that they have the skills and experiences that equip them to lead GREAT instruction in their schools.

In addition, you have to train assistant principals regularly. In many schools, the assistant principals assist in leading the day-to-day work of their school's special education department. They also help set the agenda for the regular faculty meetings and assist in designing the school-based professional development activities. The assistant principals are often the official supervisor for particular staff members, perhaps including special education teachers and paraprofessionals. They are also future principals. By investing in the assistant principals, you will impact the instructional program for students with disabilities now as well as in the future.

I often run into special education administrators who say that they cannot get on the agenda of their monthly principals' or assistant principals' meetings. I know the problem. They have not done all of the work needed to set a strong foundation for this work.

They have not developed deep partnerships and ongoing collaboration with the folks at the central office. They have not analyzed the data and shown a fresh insight into student performance across the district. They have not partnered with the curriculum and instruction department to help expand their work so that the instructional initiatives are broad and inclusive of students with disabilities. They have not dropped into their central office colleagues' offices regularly to hear about their priorities and provide insight on how those priorities can be tinkered with in order to cast a wider net for all children. If you are having a difficult time getting on the agenda for the regular principals' meetings, consider how you can build a strong foundation to garner some great momentum.

If the agenda setters for those principals' and assistant principals' meetings don't think your message is important enough to share, perhaps you have not done the groundwork to develop a message. All of the relationship building, data analyses, and true partnerships develop a ground game where other decision makers see the great value in your work and priorities because your work and priorities represent their work and priorities.

That monthly meeting is critical, but it is not the only option for training. In fact, ongoing training and support includes a variety of activities. It is critical that you participate in that monthly formal meeting, but it is equally important that you take advantage of other times that principals are gathered in order to spread your message and provide training, coaching, and support.

Lastly, and perhaps most importantly, visit the principals in their schools. Set up meetings with the principals to ask how you can provide support. You can use that time to reinforce your overall message, but the purpose is not to demand action. It is to build relationships, be responsive, *and* to continue the specific messages you have regarding GREAT instruction.

> **The thing about fighting fires is this. If you spend all of your time fighting fires, then you will *always* spend all of your time fighting fires.**

If you only show up when there is a problem, you are not a real partner. You are a firefighter. The thing about fighting fires is this: If you spend all of your time fighting fires, you will *always* spend all of your time fighting fires. You have to invest your time toward proactive actions, like visiting principals in their schools for proactive discussions, not just reactive firefighting.

Don't Rely on Muscle

On occasion, I hear a central office staff member say, "Who is going to make the principals do this?" When I hear that, I know we have a problem. I have to help that employee grow and evolve to a more advanced level of thinking. As I mentioned before, authority isn't all it is cracked up to be. If you "make" someone do something, you will probably only get obligatory compliance, not true ownership.

The employee who makes that statement is not being self-reflective. If you are asking principals or other school personnel to implement an instructional initiative or practice and they don't, you have to figure out why. Very often, the reason does not reflect the lack of priorities or effort of the principal, but something is off regarding what they are being asked to do.

It could be that there are too many messages bombarding the principals and they can't focus on any one. It could be that the different departments in the central office are not aligned. It could be that a string of initiatives have come and gone and there is little confidence that the newest work will make the long haul.

There could also be other barriers. Perhaps the instructional activity or initiative being proposed is not well-grounded in research or it doesn't respond to the needs that principals perceive as most critical. Perhaps there was a very quick presentation of the new activities and an all too quick adoption of the work. If you want to implement instructional practices that are implemented and sustained over time, you have to involve principals and others into the choice of the work. Then, you have to build ongoing systems of support, brainstorming, encouragement, training, and monitoring.

All this to say, you can't rely on muscle to systematically move your district forward. If you find yourself promoting initiatives or activities that are not taking, the solution is typically *not* to tighten the screws. If very few people are following you, you are not leading.

If, on the other hand, you get a majority of folks to follow your direction with a few dissenters, then you have built a strong foundation for change. On occasion, authority needs to be used for those few holdouts if the momentum is seen across the district, but if you are getting few takers, re-think your approach.

Guiding Questions

- After reviewing the considerations above, which instructional practices will you implement during the first year of implementation (or the next year of implementation if you have already started)?

- Have you developed deep partnerships with principals that go beyond responding to the occasional fire? If your answer is "yes," provide examples of how you have done that.

- Do principals in your school district have the perception that the special education work is an isolated component with relation to their work, or do they consider the support and messaging from the special education department to be a critical component of their overall school improvement efforts? Support your answer.

- Do you provide ongoing training to principals and assistant principals during their regular district meetings? Why or why not? If not, is it because you haven't invested in laying the foundation at the central office and with principals? If that is the case, how can you change that?

- At your core, do you have the perspective that you could make a difference in your school district if someone would "make the principals do it"? Does the central office special education department have that perspective? If so, are you willing to shift your thinking toward becoming a change agent?

- During your time as a special education leader, have you had success in changing the practices of principals? If so, how did you do it? If not, what should you change regarding your approach? (Truthfully, your answer may include both "yes" and "no." If that is the case, explain the differences in your approaches that fostered different results.)

XIV
Step 8: Invest Deeply in the School-Based Coaches Who Will Provide Ongoing Training

Here is where we really start to have an impact on the instructional practices that are taking place in the schools. It might be surprising that we haven't discussed training teachers yet. We have spent a great amount of attention on making sure the district is in alignment and the overall context is ready to support this work.

Again, why so much time on the context? How many initiatives—many times, competing initiatives—have come and gone during your time in the field of education? Tons. Many of them have never actually had an impact on what happens in classrooms. We don't want this work to add to that list. We have invested deeply in the relationships and training needed to set the context.

Now we have to remember our illustration with Elisha in the martial arts scenario. She will never reach her goal if she doesn't practice, receive coaching and feedback, and become enmeshed with a group of folks who are working on the same goal. We have to create those experiences for our teachers (both general education and special education) if we are going to consistently see implementation of our research-based instructional practices.

How do we do that? We must enable folks who work in the schools to become the instructional coaches for this work—just like Elisha has a coach who organizes and provides feedback during her workouts. The hard question: Who are those folks in your schools? Depending on your district, you might have special education personnel who are responsible for supporting the special education work in various schools. They might be referred to as lead teachers for special education, special education lead teachers, etc. In some school districts, those folks do not have teaching duties. In other districts, there are special education personnel, perhaps called department chairs, who have some teaching duties, but also get some extra planning time during the day to support the school-wide special education program.

If you don't have those folks in your district, you might need to rely on various personnel who act as instructional coaches whose job it is to provide support, training, and coaching to teachers as they implement refined teaching practices. Even if you don't have the special education-specific personnel described in the previous paragraph, you should still very much include the instructional coaches in your building who can help design and drive this work at their assigned schools.

Whoever you consider your school-based instructional support people, you must invest deeply in them. One training at the beginning of the school year is insufficient. They must have deep knowledge in two big areas: how to implement the specific instructional practices with fidelity and, just as important, how to change adult practices in their schools so that the practices are implemented consistently across general and special education environments.

At a minimum, you should pull those folks together at least two times a month for ongoing training, coaching, and brainstorming. They must have the opportunity to discuss their next monthly steps in their respective schools, but perhaps more importantly, they need the opportunity to share with each other and benefit from their colleagues' experiences.

Remember in the martial arts illustration how Elisha must work with a group of like-minded folks who are pursuing the same goal? She will never reach her goal if she is only attached to a coach. Likewise, your school-based instructional leaders in this work must have colleagues who are phone calls and emails away for continued brainstorming. They must get together at least two times a month to share their experiences, victories, lessons learned, and barriers. This collegiality is almost more important than the formal trainings that will be provided during these regular sessions. There will be great power for these personnel in knowing that they are part of a larger group of folks who are building momentum and change for students. Now this is getting exciting!

Guiding Questions

- In your schools, who will provide the ongoing training and support for teachers? Describe the arrangements that will be made so that those personnel meet twice a month to receive additional training and, almost more important, brainstorm next steps for their respective schools. The meetings can be limited to 90 minutes per session.

XV

Step 9: Provide Ongoing Training, Coaching, and Opportunities for Teachers to Collaborate

This is where the rubber hits the road. At the end of the day, the only way to consistently increase student achievement is to provide GREAT instruction. The only way to do that is to enhance and change teacher practices. Again, that does not mean teachers bear all of the responsibility. They play a part, a big part. As leaders, we must also understand our obligation. That obligation applies to special education administrators, school-level leaders, and other central office personnel. Our responsibility is to create the environment, setting, training, resources, and momentum so that teachers can refine their practices.

Earlier, I shared a dated version of the umbrella standards from the National Staff Development Council (Hirsh, 2007), which is now known as Learning Forward. As I mentioned, even though the standards have changed over the years, the former version still speaks to me. If we are going to systematically change adult practices in our schools, we must impact the *context*, focus on research-based *content*, and use effective *processes*.

The first half of this book reviewed the content, the type of instruction that needs to occur. So far, in the second half, we have focused on impacting the context. You read about shifting your focus, knowing and using the data, developing deep partnerships, and creating alignment. You also read and answered questions about training principals, assistant principals, and instructional coaches (whatever their titles may be) so that those personnel are equipped to provide leadership, direction, and support to teachers.

None of those professionals, however, provide GREAT instruction in our classrooms on a daily basis. We must now systematically and strategically support our teachers so they can do our schools' most important work: teach our students.

There is some good news and bad news at this point. The good news is that after working on all of the previous steps (recognizing they are not linear), your school district will be in a powerful position to make solid next steps to improve instruction. You have shaped the context so that teachers are working in a completely aligned environment in which all personnel, including administrators and support personnel, are equipped to have a singular, focused message for teachers. With this strong underpinning, your next steps will not be a passing fad. It has the foundation to last. The bad news is that none of that will have an impact on student learning unless you complete the next steps: providing diligent and uncompromising support for your teachers so that they can refine and improve their instructional practices with fidelity. You must complete the next steps, an effective process to support teacher change. Let's jump right in.

Training Principals Turns Into Actions

You have worked to train multiple groups of people. Their training includes different components because they have different roles in providing support and leadership to teachers. For example, principals sit in a unique seat. They are the leaders of their school. They can and should delegate many duties. There are some things, however, that they must personally carry out. In order to systematically and consistently impact classroom instruction, principals must be the "The Four Letter M's" for this work.

- **Principals must be the *messenger.*** They must stand in front of their faculty repeatedly to lead this charge. They must convincingly and powerfully state that increasing the achievement of students with disabilities and other students who struggle is a top priority. In fact, across the school, there will only be a few priorities for improvement over the next couple of school years, and this work is one of them. All faculty members must commit to working together to refine their craft so that more students, including those with disabilities and those who struggle, will demonstrate increased student achievement. In fact, by being fully committed to the work of implementing GREAT instruction, all groups of students will show increased learning. Because of their position as the instructional and administrative leader across the school, principals must be the messenger.

- **Principals must be the *motivator.*** They must express great faith in their faculties and continually recognize that this is noble work. Effective principals will ensure the faculty that there will be the necessary resources to make this shift. There will be ongoing training and time for brainstorming, debriefing, and reflecting on the work. They know that every person in the school has the ability to meet this challenge head-on. The faculty can do this. Principals have faith and will be there every step of the way, working side-by-side with teachers so that they are supported and encouraged. In addition, and this is incredibly important, the principals will take some things off the plate. Since they are focusing on just a few priorities for the year, many things from other initiatives will be removed. Now that is motivating!

- **Principals must be the *monitor.*** They must ensure that there are scheduled times when teachers will be able to reflect on their implementation and move forward. Mistakes are expected and allowed. That happens anytime someone is trying something new or refining an existing skill. That is okay. At the end of the day, however, the expectation is that all members of the faculty are committed to planning together, making attempts at incorporating the universal and specially designed instruction within GREAT instruction, determining if the practices are having a positive impact on student learning, and then refining their efforts. The principals will work with other administrators and teacher leaders to build systems in which teacher and student progress are monitored routinely.

- **Principals must be the *muscle*.** They must set an extremely positive and safe tone where teachers are allowed to improve their skills. They must focus on encouraging and supporting teachers. Make no mistake, however. These actions are required. There might be some faculty members who are not willing to move forward with this work. Therefore, the principals must be the muscle and have individual conversations with specific staff members, perhaps take other difficult actions.

When training is provided for principals, these roles must be explained and brainstormed. Principals should plan out how they will fill these roles for their schools. Remember how it is critically important to develop deep partnerships with principal supervisors? This is when that partnership pans out. As special education administrators, you might not have the leverage to have this type of conversation with principals, but their supervisors can. They can train and explain to principals how to be true leaders in this work for their respective schools.

Training Coaches Turns Into Actions

Earlier, we discussed training personnel who would provide school-level training, coaching, and support. Ideally, you will gather these personnel twice a month for training and support. During those ongoing sessions, they must be equipped to provide training in the one to three specific instructional practices that will be prioritized. They must be knowledgeable about the research and advantages behind the pedagogy. They must also be given the materials and practice needed in order to provide training with each of their school's faculties.

Much more importantly, they need to be given the skills necessary to facilitate ongoing brainstorming and reflection sessions with teachers in their assigned schools. In fact, those types of activities—if implemented routinely, perhaps twice a month in each school—are much more powerful than passive training for teachers.

Scheduling Training, Coaching, and Debriefing Sessions

In most school calendars, there are specific days for professional development activities. The students typically don't have school on those days and the faculties can participate in activities that refine their work. Before the school year even starts, some of the time on each of those days, including both pre-planning days and other professional development days, should be reserved for this work. Go ahead. Put this work on the calendar. Schedule sessions for each of the days that will be utilized to promote the identified research-based instructional practices. If you don't schedule these sessions now, you will look up several weeks into the school year and wonder what happened to the momentum and movement regarding this work. Schedule it now, or you will forget it later.

Typically, the number of designated professional development days is limited. Therefore, schools must also place other times on the schedule throughout the school year in which this work can be addressed. This can occur during grade-level meetings or other small-group meetings. At times, it can occur during school-wide faculty meetings, but much of this work should occur in smaller, more intimate discussions in which teachers work together to plan, implement, and reflect on their instruction and the impact on student learning.

Professional Development Is Not Always "Training"

When we talk about professional development, many teachers think of sitting in a large room and hearing from someone who has expertise in a particular topic. That can be useful, but it only reflects a small portion of the activities that are needed to develop professionals. Referencing back to the martial arts example, Elisha is not going to become a stronger martial artist by merely sitting in a room and hearing about effective punches and kicks. She needs to dive in and do some work.

Likewise, teachers need to spend time planning their new instructional practices, pulling together the needed materials, trying out those elements, and then reflecting on how they impact students' experiences and student learning. During those designated professional development days (including pre-planning) and other designated times, the school-based coaches must facilitate a wide variety of activities as part of "training."

If a school chooses to focus on drastically increasing practice turns and feedback for students, for example, teachers need to participate in a session that reviews the reasons why that particular practice is important and to hear about examples of that work. Then, teachers need to break into small groups and actually design how they are going to make that happen. At the elementary level, teachers can separate into grade-level groups. In the middle and high schools, they might work in subject-area groups. The point is that they need a chance to make this instructional practice their own.

They can brainstorm how every minute of the school day is drastically important, and they need to build experiences for students at every opportunity for taking practice turns and receiving feedback from their teachers, peer students, themselves, or technology. They might discuss the 15-minute homeroom period that occurs every morning. Instead of students sitting idly and listening for school-wide announcements, every teacher can have a content-related activity waiting for students.

On some mornings, a proactive math teacher can have one completed word problem posted in five locations throughout the room. He might say, "Students, last night I was completing this word problem, but I don't know if I completed it correctly. Please work in your assigned groups to review my work and determine if I completed it accurately. If I made mistakes, please write directions for me about what I did wrong and what I should have done." Do you see how the students would start their school day working collaboratively, practicing solving word problems, analyzing the teacher's response, and working together to provide guidance? Those 15-minute homeroom periods can be meaningful places where practice turns and feedback can be ramped up rather than students sitting passively and missing the opportunity for meaningful academic activities.

The point is that once teachers start brainstorming together, they will benefit from each other's ideas, encouragement, feedback, and perspectives. After addressing any "down time," like daily homeroom, teachers can then brainstorm how to drastically increase practice turns and feedback during their instructional periods. A science teacher might ask, "How can I get all students to take practice turns and receive feedback when we are working on the standards related to the periodic table?" By working together, their ideas and brainstorming will flourish.

In addition to sessions in which teachers plan and prepare for their instructional practices, they need the opportunity to work together and reflect on implementation, and perhaps most importantly, determine how student learning is being impacted. For example, "For the last couple of weeks, we all tried to drastically increase practice turns and feedback during our instruction. We agreed on using a common assessment to determine if our students were progressing in their expository writing. At today's session, let's debrief on our attempts and also discuss the impact that it had on students' experiences in the classroom and their performance."

The analysis of student data, perhaps on common assessments, is critically important. That review lays the foundation for the conversation. Are the improvements in instructional practices, such as increasing practice turns and feedback, actually making a difference in student learning? If so, keep going and improving. If not, reflect on why and make adjustments for the next attempts at the new instructional practice. The main point of this entire book is to increase student achievement. That is our gauge for success. Instead of waiting for the results of some end-of-year required assessment, teachers should work together (with facilitation from the coaches or administrators) to analyze the data and make instructional decisions based on that progress.

Do you see how everything is landing at this place, where all resources and messages are aligned and we provide the time, attention, and support so that teachers are given opportunities to work together and benefit from the corporate knowledge and expertise?

Lastly, we have to give teachers the opportunity to observe in their colleagues' classrooms. Let's make sure we understand the purpose of peer observations. It is not to evaluate or provide feedback to the teacher being observed. After significant research and efforts into what it takes to change adult practices through staff development, Joyce and Showers (2002) wrote about shifting the purpose of peer observations. It is merely to observe another teacher implementing his craft. The observing teacher can learn skills and implement those skills in her classroom. Sometimes, the observer will realize that some activities won't translate to another classroom, which is certainly acceptable. The point is that the observer is not in her colleagues' classrooms to critique the work, but to learn from it.

If we are going to provide teachers with the appropriate support to refine their practices, you must provide regularly scheduled training on new information, but, more importantly, you have to facilitate routine sessions (perhaps at least twice a month) where teachers review the impact on student learning, reflect on implementation, and make and develop activities for next steps. In addition, you must provide the opportunity for teachers to observe each other to witness their peers implementing their newly-learned practices in order to learn from other teacher's efforts.

Guiding Questions

- When you are ready to systematically assist teachers in shaping their instructional practices, how will you assist or require schools to schedule sessions during every professional development day throughout the school year? How will you assist or require schools to also schedule sessions, at least twice a month, in which teachers will reflect on their efforts, review the impact on student learning, and develop next steps for implementation?

- How often will you meet with the instructional coach personnel (regardless of their title) to provide them with ongoing brainstorming and support as they assist their schools? Will you ensure that these personnel are gathered at least twice a month? Who will lead this ongoing training of the instructional coaches? Ideally it should include members of the instruction department and the special education department.

XVI
Step 10: Follow the Timeline

Unfortunately, many leaders in school systems think they can launch a new initiative at the beginning of the school year. That will never be effective. In those places, systemic change will not occur. If you are going to effectively impact the content, context, and process needed to build truly effective instructional programs across your district (or implement any large-scale initiative), then you must start well before the beginning of the school year.

I have found that following the timeline below has resulted in systemic change that ultimately impacts classroom instruction and student achievement. This timeline is really designed for central office personnel like members of the special education department, not for school-level leaders. Their timeline will be different. In addition, this is the timeline to use if you are starting from scratch in turning the special education department from revolving around compliance and daily operations to focusing on GREAT instruction and achievement for students with disabilities.

Summer and early fall: Evaluate all statewide data (achievement, attendance, behavior). Most students typically take required statewide assessments near the end of the school year. In some places individual student results are returned to the central office and schools somewhat quickly. It takes a while longer to get district-wide results and statewide comparison data. That information may not be received until late in the summer or early fall.

As soon as any data are available, work with the data experts in your districts to format the data. It should tell a story. Looking at raw data on various spreadsheets will be cumbersome. The visual representation must be intuitive and simple to understand. Please note I am not suggesting that you wait until the state department of education releases their annual report card on schools. That will take too long. You will probably have to wait on that for the statewide comparison data. Before that time, you should work with partners in your district to format your district's data. Remember, don't just use one year of data. You must build trend data over time.

Once the data is formatted, work with your partners in schools and the central office to begin to analyze the data. What does it tell you? How has the performance of all students and students with disabilities performed over time? Are you seeing an increase across content areas and grade levels? If not, which trends are moving upward and which trends are moving downward?

As mentioned earlier, you need comparison points whenever you analyze data. Just because there is an upward movement, it may not be steep enough. You should compare your slope of progress to the state's slope for all students and students with disabilities. If, for example, you had an increase of five points in the percentage of students with disabilities who met expectations on the fifth-grade science exam and the state had an increase of 15 points, then you have a problem. You lost ground in comparison to the state.

Likewise, if the performance of students with disabilities across the state saw a decrease because of a new curriculum or new, more rigorous assessments, then you should compare your decrease to that of the statewide disability group.

The point of analyzing the data with other central office personnel is that you want to develop common conclusions regarding the data. This depth of analysis with other personnel at the central office will help develop priority areas for improvement.

Late fall: Get all central office personnel to develop a unified and common understanding of the priority elements of GREAT instruction. Once you have analyzed the data with your colleagues and drawn conclusions for the priority areas for improvement, you must develop a common understanding of the particular instructional practices that you want to see in classrooms. This is when you determine the one to three instructional practices that should be seen across the district that will have a significant impact on all students—both students with disabilities and their peers without disabilities.

You may decide to focus on effective vocabulary instruction, a balanced approach to mathematics instruction, or explicit instruction. Regardless of what you choose, now is the time to develop a consensus among all members of the instruction department as well as the special education department. The investment in this step will pay off so that teachers are not receiving mixed messages from different personnel from the central office. Even though I have not stated it explicitly, it is important to include select principals and teachers in this step. You will find a much greater receptivity to change if school-based personnel are involved in all of these steps.

January through April: Provide ongoing training, brainstorming, and debriefing to principals, assistant principals, coaches, etc. During this four-month period, your training begins. You must equip principals, assistant principals, and the school-based personnel who will provide ongoing training and coaching to lead this work. If your district provides monthly training for each of these groups, you must get on the agenda for those sessions.

This is not one-and-done. You must have sequential trainings over several months in order to not only provide awareness training, but also dig deeply into each of the priority instructional practices. It is best if the training is co-led by members of the curriculum and instruction department and the special education department. The purpose of the training is not only to review the characteristics of the priority instructional practices, but also to equip each of those audiences to fulfill their role in this work. The principals will need to be the messenger, motivator, monitor, and muscle. The assistant principals will echo the roles of the principals while also digging deeper into leading implementation. The coaching personnel will be trained to lead the ongoing small group sessions with teachers.

All of the personnel will know the work of the other groups and, in fact, share some of the work. The principals, for example, should lead some small-group teacher sessions. That will send a very clear message. With his or her other responsibilities, he will not be able to lead all training. In fact, most of that work will be led by the school-level coaches.

All of the training sessions with principals, assistant principals, and coaches should include active learning. For example, after the characteristics of the instructional practices are reviewed, the different groups can work on building out the evaluation components that will be used to monitor teachers' growth. If your district has a common teacher evaluation process, how will it be adjusted to reflect the desired teacher practices for each of the priority practices? That hands-on work will allow for great conversations and clarifying of what principals, assistant principals, and coaches should see in classrooms.

January through April: Assist the principals with structural changes that need to occur, such as school scheduling, personnel allotments, etc. for the following school year. I have often said that each new school year starts in January. That is when leaders must continue with the current school year while also strategically planning for the upcoming year. During the second semester, some schools might need to prepare for structural changes for next year.

If one of your priority instructional practices includes increasing the number and effectiveness of co-teaching classes, then you will have to assist schools in determining the needs of their students with disabilities, conduct IEP meetings that include more co-teaching classes, and schedule the classes to make it all happen. That must occur during the second semester. You can't wait until the summer. In addition, you might find that some schools have an excess of special education personnel whereas some might need more teachers. The staff allotments must occur in the spring in preparation for the start of school.

March and April: Plan summer training for teachers that is differentiated and offered multiple times over the summer to allow for different vacation schedules. During the summer, you launch training for your teachers, but that takes planning. In March and April, you must develop the schedule for that training, repeating it many times over the summer.

Teachers absolutely need and deserve their summer break. They certainly do 12 months' worth of work every year; they just do it in about 10 months. The summer gives them the time to rejuvenate, reflect on the previous school year, and plan for their new students. You should repeat the training sessions several times over the summer to allow for previously scheduled vacations and obligations. In one school district, we planned 10 different sessions of the same training during the summer. The teachers could register for the session that met their schedule.

Teachers should typically attend two sessions of the training, perhaps a half-day of training for each session. After you go beyond three hours of training, the law of diminishing returns sets in. If teachers attend one half-day of training earlier in their summer break and a refresher that goes deeper a little later on, they will be ready to start the school year and attempt the new instructional practices.

In early March, you need to send out the training schedule and open registration. If you construct your registration process carefully, you can electronically pull the list of participants in April to ensure that all schools are represented and sufficient numbers of general education and special education teachers are participating. Since you have spent a few months engaging in training with the principals, they can promote the importance of the summer training for all teachers, not just special education teachers.

In the summer, you should provide a healthy stipend for teachers' participation. Teachers should get paid for their training time. In addition, many of them will have to pay for child care expenses during the summer. A stipend will ease that burden. In some states, you will have to follow the agreements provided between your district and the respective teachers union or professional organization.

June: Provide many opportunities for the teachers to participate in the training. All central office personnel should support or directly lead the training. The training occurs during the summer. Remember, this work will be more impactful if it is not seen coming solely from the special education department. The trainers should include a variety of personnel from the instruction department and the special education department. Some trainings might be led by a special education coordinator and the science coordinator for the district. Other trainings might be led by the English/language arts coordinator and a special education lead teacher.

The trainings can be math- or ELA-specific, for example, with the teachers choosing the training that reflects their job duties. This would be especially important at the middle- and high-school levels. The secondary teachers want to attend training that is directly related to the standards they must teach. Therefore, training for high school teachers of algebra should be led by someone who has expertise in math education and a person who is accomplished in the field of special education. The content of the training should specifically address the standards that are taught in the algebra courses while utilizing the priority research-based instructional practices.

Even though principals have participated in training during the spring, they should also attend trainings during the summer. By participating with their teachers, they will be equipped to be leaders in their schools.

Pre-planning: Provide information and activities to schools to remind school personnel about the instructional priorities. Pre-planning is usually misnamed. Unfortunately, teachers are not given lots of time to plan their school year. There are plenty of meetings and required trainings. In addition, special education personnel are extremely busy with students who are moving into the school district or unexpectedly transferring between schools. Pre-planning is really a mad dash.

With all that being said, it is critically important that the priority instructional practices are re-visited during pre-planning. If not, all of the efforts over the last several months will be wasted. We have to have a booster and remind personnel that one of the biggest priorities of the school year is to systematically implement priority instructional practices that will be beneficial for all students, including students with disabilities.

The principal must stand in front of the faculty and be the messenger and motivator. This work is important and it is needed. The assistant principal and school-level coaches must provide a refresher training and share the schedule for those ongoing teacher brainstorming and reflection meetings. The training and discussions should be motivating and fun. The school year should start with great excitement and it must include a booster to the priority instructional practices.

Throughout the school year: Align all trainings, meetings, coaching, and evaluation systems to focus on the instructional practices. Expect school-based reflections, PLCs, etc. I won't give this section sufficient attention because it has been covered throughout the second half of this book. All year long, the priority instructional practices must stay on the front burner. The rapid pace of schooling cannot allow the school or district to lose focus.

At every principal meeting and assistant principal meeting throughout the school year, there should be some time, perhaps only 30 minutes per monthly meeting, where the priorities are re-visited. The school-level administrators are so busy during the year that they often don't have time to collaborate with one another. Those meetings can become reflection and brainstorming meetings, with systematic facilitation, in which the leaders of the various schools can discuss how their ongoing training, support, and teacher sessions are shaping instructional practices across the school.

They can discuss barriers they are facing and ask their colleagues for advice. They can share what they are observing in classrooms and the progress students are making or not making. They can discuss how they are applying the teacher evaluation process, which includes a reflection on the implementation of the new instructional practices. Personnel from the curriculum and instruction department and the special education department can co-lead this work and demonstrate how it is impacting all teachers and all students, but the tremendous value in monthly meetings for principals and assistant principals is the opportunity for the leaders to brainstorm, reflect, and share together.

At the school level, this work must be continued diligently. At the regular faculty meetings, the principal can brag on those personnel who have been implementing the instructional practices effectively. In addition, teachers participate in ongoing training and those twice-a-month teacher brainstorming sessions. The only way to keep the momentum going is to continually work on refining implementation through consistent effort and collaboration.

Each school's leadership team should also discuss implementation regularly. On the common formative assessments administered throughout the school, are there indications that the instructional improvements are impacting student learning? Are there teachers who should be promoted as models? Are there teachers who need more support, encouragement, or even pressure? This work must be revisited routinely and regularly by the school's leadership team.

Guiding Questions

- How will you schedule this work? Collaborate with your district special education leadership team to develop a general schedule of activities that you will complete during each step of the timeline listed above. Who do you need to collaborate with? How will you do that? When will you do that? What indicators will you look for to indicate that you are on schedule and making systemic change during the preparation, collaboration, and implementation stages? Be specific enough in your schedule that you see a clear path, but also be open to modifying your schedule as you move along. Also, be sure to plan those informal moments and discussions with colleagues that will move the ball forward. If that means you have to drop into other leaders' offices, then put it on your schedule to remind yourself to do so. If you don't have it written down, it won't happen.

XVII
You Always Knew

This book started with a meeting with your superintendent and a directive: "We have to drastically increase the achievement of students with disabilities. What should we do?" We have to provide GREAT instruction in every class, in every school, for every child, every day.

The truth is, you already knew that. You may have forgotten as you spent time as a special education administrator. The demands of compliance and daily operations might have become the major focus of your work. But deep in your heart, you knew that the school factor with the greatest impact on student learning is the instruction that is provided.

When you were a teacher, you worked tirelessly to continually refine your instruction to support your students. You reflected on lessons and units that had great impact. You also reviewed those activities that weren't so successful. As a teacher, you knew that if you created engaging, exciting, and effective pedagogy, you could have a tremendous impact on students. You could change lives.

Now is the time to get back to that belief. It must center your work. Over time, you have developed many more skills. You have a deep understanding of compliance and daily operations—lessons learned from your years as an administrator. Hopefully, after reading this book, your skillset has grown even further. You have a structure and frame in place to outline specific instructional practices that will set the foundation for specially designed instruction. You also have a greater understanding of the partnerships, context, and ongoing activities you must build to systematically change adult practices for the long term.

This work is hard. There is no getting around that. But it is noble. That deserves repeating. Your work is noble. You have the opportunity to change the lives of students with disabilities and many other students through GREAT instruction and powerful leadership. You can do this.

References

Archer, A. L. & Hughes, C. A. (2011). *Explicit instruction: Effective and efficient teaching.* New York: Guilford Press.

Brown, L. (2004). Personal communication with the author.

Dean, C. B., Hubbell, E. R., Pitler, H., & Stone, B. (2013). *Classroom instruction that works: Research-based strategies for increasing student achievement* (2nd ed.). Alexandria, VA: Association for Supervision and Curriculum Development.

Education for All Handicapped Children Act – P.L. 94-142 (1975). 94th Congress of the United States.

Eggers, L. (1993). Personal communication with the author.

Every Student Succeeds Act – P.L. 114-95. (2015). 114th Congress of the United States.

Friend, M. & Burrello, L. C. (2005). *Power of 2* (2nd ed.) [DVD]. United States: A Forum on Education.

Fuchs, D. & Fuchs, L. S. (2005). Peer-assisted learning strategies: Promoting word recognition, fluency, and reading comprehension in young children. *The journal of special education, 39*(1), pp. 34-44. Retrieved from http://files.eric.ed.gov/fulltext/EJ693939.pdf

Georgia Department of Education (2011). *Response to intervention: Georgia's student achievement pyramid of interventions.* Retrieved from www.gadoc.org/Curriculum-Instruction-and-Assessment/Curriculum-and-Instruction/Documents/RTI%20document%20Full%20Text.pdf

Hardin, J. (2014). Personal communication with the author.

Hattie, J. (2008). *Visible learning: A synthesis of over 800 meta-analyses relating to achievement.* New York: Routledge.

Hattie, J. & Yates, G. (2013). *Visible learning and the science of how we learn.* New York: Routledge.

Hirsh, S. (2007). NSDC standards and tools help strength staff development. *SEDL Letter, XIX*(1). Retrieved from www.sedl.org/pubs/sedl-letter/v19n01/nsdc-standards-tools.html

Individuals with Disabilities Education Act – P.L. 101-476 (1990). 101st Congress of the United States.

Individuals with Disabilities Education Act – P.L. 105-17 (1997). 105th Congress of the United States.

Individuals with Disabilities Education Improvement Act – 108-446 (2004). 108th Congress of the United States.

Marzano, R. J., Pickering, D. J., & Pollock, J. E. (2001). *Classroom instruction that works: Research-based strategies for increasing student achievement.* Alexandria, VA: Association for Supervision and Curriculum Development.

Marzano, R. J. (2004). *Building background knowledge for academic achievement.* Alexandria, VA: Association for Supervision and Curriculum Development.

National Institute of Child Health and Human Development (2000). *National Reading Panel. Teaching children to read: An evidence-based assessment of the scientific research literature on reading and its implications for reading instruction: Reports of the subgroups.* Washington, DC: U.S. Government Printing Office.

National Mathematics Advisory Panel. (2008). *Foundations for success: The final report of the national mathematics advisory panel.* Washington, DC: U.S. Department of Education.

No Child Left Behind Act – P.L. 107-110. (2001). 107th Congress of the United States.

O'Connor, J. L. (2009). *Turning average instruction into great instruction: School's leadership's role in student achievement.* Lanham, MA: Rowman & Littlefield.

O'Connor, J. L. (2010). *Students with disabilities can meet accountability standards: A road map for school leaders.* Lanham, MA: Rowman & Littlefield.

O'Connor, J. L. (2012). Million dollar question. *In CASE, 53*(3), pp. 3-4. Retrieved from http://casecec.org/Documents/InCASE/Vol53_No3_Jan-Mar2012.pdf

O'Connor, J. L. (2013). Guiding questions for addressing suspension disproportionality. *In CASE, 54*(4), pp. 18-19. Retrieved from http://casecec.org/Documents/InCASE/Vol54_No4_Apr-Jun2013.pdf

O'Connor, J. L., Primm, B. & Stancil, B. (2006). *Cross-age peer tutoring using direct instruction as a Tier 2 intervention for non-responders.* Unpublished paper.

O'Connor, S. (1998). Personal communication with the author.

U.S. Department of Education. (2014). *36th annual report to Congress on the implementation of the Individuals with Disabilities Act, 2014.* Retrieved from www2.ed.gov/about/reports/annual/osep/2014/index.html

Villa, A., Thousand, J., & Nevin, A. (2013). *A guide to co-teaching: New lessons and strategies to facilitate student learning* (3rd ed.). Thousand Oaks, CA: Corwin Press.

Wall, M. (2015). Personal communication with the author.

Woods, R. (2016). *Student attendance: Changing the conversation. Georgia Department of Education.* Retrieved from www.gadoe.org/External-Affairs-and-Policy/Policy/Documents/Student%20Attendance%20and%20Student%20Achievement%20Updated%20March%202016.pdf

Other Books by John L. O'Connor

Student with Disabilities Can Make AYP: What Every School Leader Should Know

Turning Average Instruction into Great Instruction: School Leadership's Role in Student Achievement

Students with Disabilities Can Meet Accountability Standards: A Roadmap for School Leaders

About the Author

John O'Connor has led school improvement initiatives at the state and local levels during his 26 years in public education. He started as a special education teacher of students with orthopedic impairments at the elementary and middle-school levels. Since that time, John has served as Program Manager with the Georgia Department of Education and served in multiple leadership capacities in various local school districts. He has been an Assistant Director for Special Education, Executive Director for Special Services, and Assistant Superintendent for Student Services. Currently, he leads the Multi-Tiered System of Supports with the Henry County School System, a district about 40 minutes south of Atlanta, Georgia. John has over 20 publications including this book, his fourth. His previous books include: *Students with Disabilities Can Make AYP, Turning Average Instruction into GREAT Instruction* and *Students with Disabilities Can Meet Accountability Standards.* John has provided training to over 400 local, state, and national audiences. He lives in Stockbridge, Georgia, with his two teenage sons, J.T. and Luke. John can be reached at greatinstruction@bellsouth.net.